MW01617813

# OUR JEWISH ROOTS

## A CATHOLIC WOMAN'S GUIDE TO FULFILLMENT TODAY BY CONNECTING WITH HER PAST

CHERYL DICKOW

Other books by Cheryl Dickow include:

- *Elizabeth: A Holy Land Pilgrimage*
- *Raising Christian Children in a Secular World*
- *Seven Essential Goals of a Godly Woman*
- *Mary ~ Ever Virgin, Full of Grace*

To ask Cheryl to speak at your event contact her at
Cheryl@BezalelBooks.com
or to find the finest in Catholic fiction and non-fiction visit:

**www.BezalelBooks.com**

Printed in the United States of America



---

A number of times throughout this book I reference, or quote from, one of my all-time favorite books: *The Privilege of Being a Woman* by Alice von Hildebrand; Sapientia Press of Ave Maria University; 2007. Mrs. Von Hildebrand inspires me be to all that I can be as a woman; I believe her words will inspire you as well.

---

ISBN 978-0-9823388-8-9
Library of Congress Control Number 2010904317

# *Foreword*

When Cheryl invited me to have an advance look at Our Jewish Roots and honored me with the opportunity to share my thoughts on the book, I was honored and humbled. As a fan of Cheryl's writing for years, I can honestly say that her book Elizabeth: A Holy Land Pilgrimage had a profound impact upon me spiritually, professionally and personally. The Old Testament values and traditions that Cheryl so eloquently imparted into that work of fiction spoke to my soul, encouraging me to look into the roots of our Catholic faith.

While I spend my days embracing the latest in technological advances and employing them in responding to the call to New Evangelization, I also firmly recognize and love the time honored teachings and traditions of our faith. This recognition and appreciation has been enhanced over the years by my friendship with a wonderful group of women from our local Jewish temple. Our first acquaintances happened on the playground when our children were toddlers, and have been nurtured over the past several years as we meet bimonthly for a rousing game of Mahj Jongg, a tile game that is popular among Jewish women. As the only Catholic woman in a group of six Mahj mavens, I have had a unique classroom for learning some of the Jewish roots of our Catholic faith.

Over the past fifteen years, I have undressed the Torah at my best friend's son's Bar Mitzvah, dined in a family Sukkot, and prayed Mourner's Kaddish with a dear friend who became a widow far too soon. I have had a front row seat to their family celebrations of traditional Jewish feasts and watched their calendar of holidays unfold as a compliment to our Catholic liturgical calendar, intersecting at key points of the year. Watching these women provide faith training for their sons and daughters in a city without many Jewish families has helped me recommit to my role as primary religious educator in my own domestic church.

With Our Jewish Roots, Cheryl Dickow has given Catholic women the gift of learning to treasure many of the teachings of our Catholic Church within the context of their Jewish traditions. Exploring such important topics as True Feminism, Theology of the Body, the role of silent prayer, and the concept of Avodah in our vocations, Cheryl has provided a rich backdrop for these important expressions of the fullness of our faith.

By introducing us to strong Old Testament heroines such as Noah's wife, Rebekka and Deborah, and inviting us to intimately know their lives, Cheryl has given every Catholic woman a unique peek into our heritage.

As a wife, a mother, and a Catholic woman, I would like to personally thank Cheryl for this wonderful book, Our Jewish Roots. I know that it will be a transformational read for so many of us. With great care and attention to detail, and in a compelling fashion, she has gifted us with a reminder of the very roots of the faith we hold so dear and has reminded us of the scriptural gems that can and should support and encourage us every day. I am convinced that Cheryl's work will be a "mitzvah" for many of us, an act of kindness and support that will help us to strengthen the foundations of our faith while we prepare for whatever the future holds for us.

Lisa M. Hendey<br>
Founder and Editor of www.CatholicMom.com<br>
best-selling author<br>
*The Handbook for Catholic Moms:*<br>
*Nurturing Your Heart, Mind, Body and Soul*

Dearest Sister-in-Christ,

I write this book with the full and complete belief that our lives are more beautiful, more bountiful, than the world would like us to believe. It is also my firm belief that we are indebted to our Jewish heritage in ways that we often don't understand, imagine, or recognize.

So before you begin the study of the women from our faith's history, I invite you to read a few ways in which our Jewish roots have come to fruition through the life, death and resurrection of our Savior. I hope you will enjoy learning about the roots of such things as our baptism, mysticism or why a name is so important.

Once you begin the study of women, I encourage you to take the time to learn the Scripture suggested with each woman's story, and to come to a very real understanding of your own beauty and dignity as a daughter of the King who comes from a line of incredible women. As Catholic women we have the ultimate family tree! I believe that in connecting with your past you will be most fully alive today. My prayer for you is that the realization of God's truth in your life be full and complete so that your existence, while pleasing to Him, is also pleasing to yourself.

You will notice that each section begins with an excerpt from the truly anointed document by John Paul II, *Mulieris Dignitatem.* It is a document on the dignity and vocation of women and is well worth reading in its entirety. It is on the Vatican's website. John Paul II made an historic journey to Israel and prayed at the Wailing Wall and has indicated his great respect for our Jewish heritage. In shepherding us, John Paul II was instrumental in teaching us to look ahead but also encouraged us to stay connected to our rich and meaningful past.

*Cheryl Dickow*

*Traditions*

*Teachings*

*and*

*Truths*

*Rooted*

*in the*

*Jewish Faith*

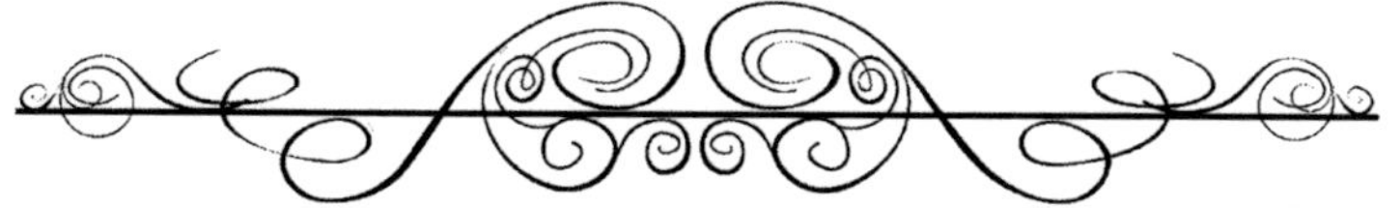

## *The Matriarchs of the Faith*

Sarah, Rebekah, Rachel, and Leah, often called The Matriarchs of the Faith, provide a remarkable insight into God's commitment to women and His interest in how women play an integral part in His plan for mankind. These women teach us both about the roots of our faith but also how our faith has unfolded so that we, as Christian women today, can live more fully for Christ. We learn from these women how to be better in all aspects of our life because we understand that His promises to us are unshakable.

Sarah was a woman whose life's goal was to have a child. She was married to Abraham; the Talmud teaches that along with Abraham, Sarah was a great converter of people to the monotheistic religion of Judaism. She is credited with saving many souls as she converted innumerable people from their pagan beliefs to monotheism. Additionally, Sarah's own faith was such that she accompanied Abraham as he answered God's call to leave Ur and journey to the promised land. Abraham heard directly from God but Sarah relied on faith alone to make the journey and thus won great favor from God. Her faith was an admirable and necessary quality as she was to be the woman to whom countless generations would be born. Ultimately Sarah, at the remarkable age of ninety, does give birth to a son, Isaac.

Sarah's beloved son Isaac grows into a young man who marries Rebekah. We see, quite pointedly in Scripture, that Isaac's marriage to Rebekah occurs very near to the time of Sarah's death. Rebekah is meant to carry Sarah's mantle and continue the line of the Matriarchs. Rebekah is a devoted wife and hers is a marriage filled with loving kindness. Through Sarah's marriage to Abraham and Rebekah's marriage to Isaac we are shown the great value God puts upon the union of a man and a woman and how they are meant to work, as partners, towards His goals.

Rebekah gives birth to twins, Esau and Jacob. Jacob falls in love with Rachel but is tricked into marrying her older sister, Leah. Although Jacob eventually marries Rachel as well, it is Leah to whom God

continually blesses as Leah gives birth to more than half of the men to whom the tribes of Israel will issue. The Talmud teaches that each sister, Rachel and Leah, brings a particular aspect of the divine feminine into the lineage of God's people. It is Rachel who cries out from the heavens, generations later, as Pharaoh slaughters infant Hebrew baby boys in Egypt while it is Leah who steadfastly becomes the mother of many of the tribes of Israel.

## *Marriage Vows and Covenantal Relationships*

The nuptial covenant between God and his people Israel had prepared the way for the new and everlasting covenant in which the Son of God, by becoming incarnate and giving his life, has united to himself in a certain way all mankind saved by him, thus preparing for "the wedding-feast of the Lamb." ~ *Catechism of the Catholic Church* 1612

What great reassurance we receive when Christ calls Himself our bridegroom! Of course this can only be truly comforting—and reveal the depth of His commitment—when we understand the context within which He spoke. We cannot look at the lack of marital commitment in today's world, whether Jewish or Christian, and fully grasp what Jesus meant when He answered the question about fasting by saying, "*Can the wedding guests mourn as long as the bridegroom is with them? The days will come when the bridegroom is taken away from them, and then they will fast.*" Matthew 9:15.

What did Christ want us to understand when He used that term bridegroom? Isaiah offers a very clear understanding of the wedded relationship Jesus would have been speaking of when He proclaimed Himself the bridegroom to us, His Church and bride. Along with the words He used to portray the union between Himself and us, His bride, Christ also used the Wedding at Cana to further clarify the idea that our relationship with Him was as indissoluble as a marriage vow.

Even today, a Jewish wedding ceremony continues to draw upon the marital covenant Christ spoke of and as is found in Isaiah 54:5, "*For he who has become your husband is your Maker; his name is the Lord of hosts; Your redeemer is the Holy One of Israel, called God of all the earth.*"

To begin with, both the Jewish bride and her bridegroom are typically walked down the aisle by their respective parents. In that way there is a real sense of the context of Genesis 2:24, "*That is why a man leaves his father and mother and clings to his wife, and the two of them become one body.*" It is a visual expression of that 'leaving of parents' and joining together as one.

When the couple join together, in front of God and man, it is under a chupah, which is an open, four-sided canopy structure that has many meanings but most closely symbolizes the first home that the bride and groom share, is reminiscent of the tent of Abraham and Sarah, and is open sided to indicate the welcoming of friends and family just as Abraham welcomed the angels who foretold of Sarah's upcoming pregnancy.

A Jewish marriage is, itself, contractual in nature and the actual contract is called a ketubah. Just as God's covenantal contract with Abraham required circumcision and Moses' covenantal contract was sealed with blood upon an altar, so, too, the ketubah requires something from each party. Remember that God's covenant with Noah also involved a sign from God, a rainbow, in recognition of the promise.

Our God is a God of covenants; so, when two people enter into a Jewish marriage, their union is contractual, or covenantal, with each bringing to the union a promise of love, fidelity, support in difficult times, as well as joy in all things.

The Jewish bride, also known as the kallah, wears a badeken, or veil. The veil covers the young bride's face to symbolize that physical beauty is a thing of passing and that what truly matters is the soul and modesty of the bride; both hallmarks of Jewish tradition that

hearken back to Rebekah's meeting with Isaac. This is both acceptable and welcomed by the husband because he wants to show that his commitment to his bride is not dependent on her physical attributes but on her inner beauty. The things of God unite the bride and groom.

Another significant part of the Jewish ceremony is the breaking of a glass. Again, this is a custom that has deep roots and is believed to have a variety of meanings associated with it; but one of the more significant symbols is to declare that the marriage will last until the glass is put back together. Which is to say, of course, that the marriage will last forever.

When Christ promises to be our bridegroom, then, He is including all these understandings for He is linking the Old Covenant with the New Covenant as the fulfillment of Jeremiah 31:31-33, "*The days are coming, says the Lord, when I will make a new covenant with the house of Israel and the house of Judah. It will not be like the covenant I made with their fathers the day I took them by the hand to lead them forth from the land of Egypt; for they broke my covenant and I had to show myself their master, says the Lord. But this is the covenant which I will make with the house of Israel after those days, says the Lord. I will place my law within them, and write it upon their hearts; I will be their God, and they shall be my people.*"

Consider, also, the Wedding at Cana, in which Christ turned ceremonial washing water into wine. It is no coincidence that He chose this sacred event, a wedding, to bring us into His fold. Reading John 2:1-12 we cannot help but feel like treasured guests witnessing what our Lord and Savior has in store for us. He who is the best wine saved for last, the blood covenant which becomes the one sacrifice that replaces the many, makes Himself known at a wedding.

When we consider Christ making Himself known as our bridegroom, we grasp the depth of those words by understanding

the original intent of marriage; the joining of a man and a woman together, forever. A union witnessed before God.

In every way, Christ has made man aware of His enduring love but none more poignantly than in describing His great love as the love that a man and a woman share in marriage. Marriage creates the place in which the "domestic church" resides and where the everyday love and commitment of a man and woman are able to mirror the same love that brought Christ to the Cross.

There is a reason that this cornerstone considers Himself a bridegroom. If any of us is called to the vocation of a Christian marriage, we are called to it with a spirit of service, love, endurance, and commitment as witnessed by Christ our bridegroom.

## *Baptismal Waters*

*In the beginning, when God created the heavens and the earth, the earth was a formless wasteland, and darkness covered the abyss, while a mighty wind swept over the waters. Genesis 1:1-2*

From the beginning, literally, the presence of God has been intimately connected to water. Water has always been life-giving and fundamental in God's plan for humans, even from the earth's very beginning as God pooled all the waters into a basin so that it, the dry land, could appear. Indeed, the image of God's breath, *Ruach*, upon the waters of Genesis, is both transforming and transfixing. It is the first action in a plan in which, ultimately, arose the sacred combination of water and word in the Baptism of Jesus in the Jordan River.

Consider, also, the second story of Genesis 2:4-7, in which it was the welling up of a stream that created the clay from which man was formed. The very idea that water is used by God to give life—or as is said in Exodus 30:20 to prevent death—is exactly why Catholics identify Baptism as the sacrament in which a person's eternal life is made available. Baptism is the Sacrament of Initiation upon which all other sacraments are able to rest. When God speaks to Moses and

instructs water to be made available to Aaron, Moses' brother and High Priest set aside for God's service, God is providing Aaron a way, specifically with the washing of his hands, to approach God at the altar. Should this way not be made available or used, Aaron will die.

We can immediately see that this ceremonial hand washing in which God uses the phrase "lest he die," is pre-figuring the baptismal waters that we must experience otherwise we, too, shall die. Of course the implication is an eternal death of our soul; a forfeiting of heavenly life with God. Like Aaron, we cannot approach God without this cleansing. Hence, Jesus' answer to Nicodemus' question, "*How can a person once grown old be born again? Surely he cannot reenter his mother's womb and be born again, can he?*" To which Jesus replies, "*Amen, amen, I say to you, no one can enter the kingdom of God without being born of water and spirit.*"

From Genesis until John the Baptist as the fulfillment of Isaiah 40:3, "*A voice cries out: In the desert prepare the way of the Lord! Make straight in the wasteland a highway for our God,*" God was preparing His people to be saved with the baptismal immersion waters John, himself set aside for this purpose, would employ in the Jordan River. It is worthwhile to note that the term "wasteland" used in Genesis 1:2 is the same term, "wasteland," used in Isaiah lending credence to the fact that until we experience the regenerative waters of baptism, we, too, live in a wasteland.

John would have used the technique for baptism as was the custom of the day at the mikvah, a full pool of water in which complete physical immersion represented a spiritual renewal and rebirth. The requirements of a mikvah, specifically, included a capacity of at least 100 gallons of fresh or spring water. Like the earth rose from the basin of water in Genesis so, too, does a person fully immerse into the mikvah waters and thus emerge anew. Certainly just as a child emerges from the life-giving amniotic fluids of his mother ready to live life in and with his family, we emerge from the life-giving waters of baptism ready to live our life in and with Christ.

Let's reflect on, however, what "ready" actually means. Even though the baby has emerged from his mother's amniotic fluids and is "ready" to join the family, this baby will need time that is filled with love, nurturance, support, knowledge, sustenance, and edification until he is ready to be a fully functioning citizen. So, too, when our babies emerge from the baptismal waters, they, also, will need love, nurturance, support, knowledge, sustenance, and edification in the ways of Christ until they are ready to live life as fully functioning Christians. Baptism is necessary to make them "ready" for their catechesis just as it creates the foundation upon which all other sacraments will build.

It is exactly for this reason that God calls us to community and why at the heart of our life as Christians is the necessity of family; because within family and then again within community we are able to contribute to the edification of one another and the eventual realization of our life in Christ. From the time of baptism until the child is able to comprehend, even in increments, the salvation that is found in Christ, a parent is obligated to contribute wholeheartedly to a child's developing faith. This is why baptism is the first of the sacraments that we are called to administer to our babies and to our converts. It creates the foundation, or more appropriately the cornerstone, from which to build our lives as Catholics. It would be negligent to withhold such a gift and would put both the baby and the parents at a disadvantage because baptism brings the Advocate, the Paraclete, with whom the Trinitarian relationship can be built up over the years.

Admittedly, the faith that is able to save us comes, for some believers, in a specific moment in time but for others of us it is a daily building up and renewing of self through the diligent practice of prayer and a daily interest in producing the fruits of the Spirit. And although baptism cannot be repeated, the life to which it calls us to is most often a daily recommitment. All of which rests upon our initiation into the faith through our baptism. As Christ says, "Whoever believes and is baptized will be saved..." When we baptize our infants we do so with the realization that this first step allows us to then fill our roles as parents, or guardians, of a life

meant for Christ; and we then embrace all of the specifics that the role demands of us, the primary transmitters of the faith. We become catechists to our children so that they build a relationship with Christ and live with an understanding of the Sacred Traditions of Catholicism.

Lumen gentium, promulgated by His Holiness Pope Paul VI on November 21, 1964, makes known the role of baptism in joining together all who follow Christ, even those not proclaiming their faith as that of Catholicism. Additionally, Lumen gentium proclaims the nature of God's call upon the people of the Old Covenant to be established as peoples of His New Covenant, through which baptism is the doorway into this new life. God answers the Gentile's eagerness to be grafted in with the sacrament of baptism.

When John the Baptist drew people to the desert with his call to repent and be baptized, he created the portal in which the Old and New Covenants were joined. The first prophet to appear in over four hundred years, John fulfilled his father's prophesy (*With the spirit and power of Elijah he will go before him, to turn the hearts of parents to their children, and the disobedient to the wisdom of the righteous, to make ready a people prepared for the Lord.* Luke 1:17) so that we, Gentiles, could take up the mantle of the New Covenant. Notice, interestingly, the word "ready" in Luke 1:17 in relation to preparation for the Lord. Baptism and repentance "make us ready" for the Lord, just as that newborn babe emerges from the mother's amniotic fluids "ready" for life. Not yet fully capable but ready for the process that will be filled with love, nurturance, support, knowledge, sustenance, and edification. Jewish teaching often considers the desert experience one that allows for clarity of purpose while also representing a cleansing and preparation for things to come. Exodus is a perfect example of a literal and spiritual desert experience. For John the Baptist, the desert experience would also have been both: literal as well as spiritual. His purpose as forerunner to Christ was crystallized as was the accomplishment of his own spiritual cleansing. John the Baptist was made "ready" in the desert.

*Teshuvah* is the Hebrew word that means "to turn around in order to return" while t*evilah b'mayim* is an immersion in water. When John the Baptist cried for repentance and baptism he was announcing the need for people to recognize their sinful ways and make a concentrated effort to do an about-face, of sorts. They had to turn around so that they could return. The visualization is quite clear. Continuing on their current paths only led away from God. God simply was not at the end of the road upon which they were traveling.

Then, once they turned around so that they could return, their return required an immersion in water. This immersion was the cleansing required after having taken the wrong road. It allowed them to start new, to start over, to begin again.

When the Catholic Church teaches that baptism washes away original sin, we understand that it is efficacious in removing the stain of the road we were put upon as a result of original sin; a road that did not lead to God but led directly away from Him and His presence. Humankind, having been forever affected by Adam and Eve, would always be required to "turn around in order to return." During Easter, we are reminded of John the Baptist's call from the desert for repentance and baptism and in renewing our own baptismal vows we find strength to continue our journeys with hope and faith in our own resurrection in Christ. He Is Risen! Alleluia!

## *Pilgrimages*

Journeying to a holy spot is something that our Jewish ancestors have always done. The Torah calls for three pilgrimages by Jewish males to Jerusalem: Passover, Shavuot, and Sukkot. Passover is the celebration of the Exodus of God's people from slavery and bondage in Egypt. Shavuot is a celebration of the first fruits of the harvest and Sukkot is the autumn remembrance of the 40 years that the Jews wandered in the desert and depended solely upon God for their food and shelter.

Even today, Matriarch Rachel's burial spot near Bethlehem is considered a sacred and holy place to which Jews make pilgrimages. Jews who journey to this burial spot spend time in deep contemplation about their history and the way in which God brought forth the 12 tribes of Israel from the Matriarchs Leah and Rachel. All such pilgrimages are meant to bind us to our Creator in unique ways and should always be seen as worth the time, effort, and sacrifice that may be involved to take such an expedition.

A pilgrimage is a journey in which there is a deep desire or interest in setting foot upon a place considered sacred and holy. Catholics have always venerated images and, in keeping with the teachings of the *Catechism of the Catholic Church*, should understand and be able to explain the difference between veneration and worship. As stated in *CCC* 2132, "*The Christian veneration of images is not contrary to the first commandment which proscribes idols. Indeed, 'the honor rendered to an image passes to its prototype,' and 'whoever venerates an image venerates the person portrayed in it.'*"

So, when a Catholic journeys to such places as the Holy Land, or even a beautiful Church in a nearby city, he or she is acting upon the way in which the Holy Spirit is able to use these places of veneration to create a deeper, more fully contemplative state than may not be otherwise attainable. In that way, a pilgrimage places a person's whole mind, body, heart, and soul at the Holy Spirit's grace and mercy.

Pilgrimages, near or far, heighten our realization of what it means to be a Catholic. Lent is a particularly perfect time where we may find it both necessary and valuable to journey to a place where our hearts will be more fully open to the message of Christ's life, death, and resurrection.

## *Angels, Messengers from Heaven*

*Mal'ach* is the Hebrew word for angels. It means "messenger." Torah has many instances in which angels interact with man to

facilitate God's will. In Genesis these instances include, but are by no means limited to, the angels who guard the gates of Eden after Adam and Eve are expelled and the angel who stops Abraham from sacrificing Isaac. Jewish teachings, like Catholic teachings, extend beyond the written word of God and this is applicable to delving into the realm of angels as well.

Since angels have always played a role in the interaction between God and man, ancient Jewish thought on their purpose has been contemplated since time immemorial. Whether acting as God's heavenly worshippers crying, "*Holy, holy, holy is the Lord of hosts!*" or delivering messages of forthcoming ruin and devastation against Sodom and Gomorrah, angels have held the fascination and rapt attention of Jewish rabbis at all points in time. Most agree that angels act as intermediaries as when an angel appears to Moses in the burning bush. Here the thought is that Moses, as righteous a man that could be found, was not yet ready to see God face to face and so God provides an angel as a necessary intermediary, showing God's great love and compassion in, once again, providing what man needs in any given circumstance.

It quite fascinating that angels may be viewed, according to some of the ancient thinkers, as working in an intermediary relationship between God and man when the task is something below or beneath God's inherent dignity or at a time when it would seem odd for God to deal with something firsthand—even though He most certainly is capable. Rabbinic teachings reflect upon this as an attempt is made to understand such instances when an omnipotent God does not Himself, let's say, reveal the news of the fate of Sodom and Gomorrah. It is interesting food for thought. Serving a monotheistic God, Jewish teaching continues to strive to understand everything within that framework. Consider how difficult it would be to fathom God wrestling with Jacob; but the idea that God would make use of an angel to bring about this necessary transformation of Jacob to Israel is easy for us mere humans to grasp.

Archangel Michael, whose name is often translated "Who is like God?" is considered to be the guardian or protector of Israel.

However, a more succinct translation of his name is actually "He who is assuredly God" coming from the Hebrew word *miykael* which is comprised of three Hebrew words: [*miy*] (who is), [*kiy*] (assuredly), and [*'el*] (God). This is why there are many Christian theologians today who study Michael with such great care, hoping to reveal his true identity and thus understand more fully Michael's role in the book of Revelation. Many of these Christian theologians contemplate if Archangel Michael is, in fact, Christ. Arguments for and against this theory abound.

Nonetheless, Archangel Michael is also considered to be the chief angel in both Old and New Testament writings. He is venerated as a soldier-angel and his feast day in the Catholic Church is September 29th. It is important to note that Michael's intercessory role in humanity seems not to have yet ended. Monte Sant'Angelo is a shrine in Italy where St. Michael is said to have appeared a number of times including during a plague in the year 1656 where a bishop invoked St. Michael's effective protection against the epidemic. From that point the site became an even more popular shrine.

Like Michael, Gabriel is a named angel in the Old Testament. Gabriel's name translates "Strength of God" and his role (I use the gender reference in the same way that our creed says *for us men and our salvation*) has always been one of deliverer of news. This is evident with the first appearance of Gabriel in the book of Daniel where Gabriel, identified by Daniel as "a manlike figure," interpreted Daniel's vision of the ram and he-goat but also in Gabriel's role in the Annunciation. Thus Gabriel, like Michael, traverses the Old and New Testament, connecting in many ways the people of the old covenant to the people of the new covenant. Saint Gabriel, along with St. Raphael, shares St. Michael's feast day of September 29th.

And while archangels hold a special place in our hearts and in our fascinations, guardian angels are also quite dear to humans. We share stories, from our firsthand knowledge, of times where we are certain our guardian angels have fulfilled their roles, *For God commands the angels to guard you in all your ways (Psalm 91:11)*

or we share stories with messages that provide great solace in the knowledge that even today God's messengers are looking out for us.

Although people cannot become angels upon death (sorry Clarence of *It's a Wonderful Life*!) this does not mean that we cannot act in a heavenly way towards our fellow man. So while we look for God's messengers to take a firsthand interest in our lives, let's remember that God always provides us with opportunities to be angelic towards one another!

### *What's in a Name?*

By the time a child is but a few years old he recognizes any number of different monikers to which he must answer. Let's take a look at fictitious Joseph James Baxter. To his grandmother he might be "Joe-Joe" while to his friends he might be "The Big J." His parents probably call him "Joe" unless they are upset and then it might become "Joseph James!" If Joe's done something really bad he quickly will become "Joseph James Baxter" while others situations that could range from being in extreme trouble to being respected by someone who doesn't know his name might find him being called "Young Man." You get the idea.

My own titles, or names, have included, but again are not limited to: Sherri, Cheryl, Cheryl Ann, Young Lady, mom, mother, Mrs. Dickow, Mrs. D., and Ma'am. Names have always played an important role in the history of mankind.

As we just looked at, many names can apply to one person. We know that when Jacob wrestled with the angel, along with a wounded hip, he acquired a new name, Israel. Additionally, we are aware of the name changes from Abram to Abraham and from Sarai to Sarah. Each of these biblical instances of name changes represents a critical piece of the story.

Significance in names also applies to the naming of children in the Bible. And while most of us skip the paragraphs of lineage where name after name is recorded, we take notice when an essential part

of the story is the selecting or giving of a name. Consider when Gabriel announces to Zechariah, "Your wife Elizabeth will bear you a son, and you shall name him John." The Hebrew name for John is *Yochanan* which means "Yahweh is gracious." So in naming this baby boy "John," people are reminded that their God, here called Yahweh, is gracious. Friends, family, and neighbors will certainly know this to be true because both Zechariah and his wife, Elizabeth, are much older and past child-bearing years. Everyone will clearly know that Elizabeth and Zechariah have been blessed with this baby **because** of Yahweh's graciousness.

All naming in the Old and New Testaments pales in comparison, though, to the giving of the one name at whose mention all knees shall bend: Jesus. And while the Son, whose name is often said to be "Yeshua" in Hebrew, is given a name that means "Salvation," it is often thought that His name can be translated "God Saves." Understanding the meaning found in a name is key to understanding why God, Himself, has so many titles.

For many Jews, and in particular Orthodox Jews, the name of God represented by the four letters Yud-Hay-Vav-Hay is never actually spoken. It is considered too sacred for man to utter. While some scholars believe that man has yet to even know the correct pronunciation of this "Tetragrammaton," as it is often called, others—along with the Church—teach that the pronunciation was lost at the time of the destruction of the temple. The High Priests would have known the correct pronunciation but in their understanding of its sacredness, would have only uttered it in the silence of their hearts.

This Tetragrammaton, or four letter name, is the name used when God identified Himself to Moses as "I AM WHO I AM;" thus identifying Himself as the Eternal One. Those scholars who believe man has never actually known the pronunciation believe this because it is without vowels and thus without indicators of pronunciation. Thus, to overcome the avoidance of uttering what could be the correct pronunciation of this too-holy name (because no one is worthy to do so), or to avoid sinfully mispronouncing this

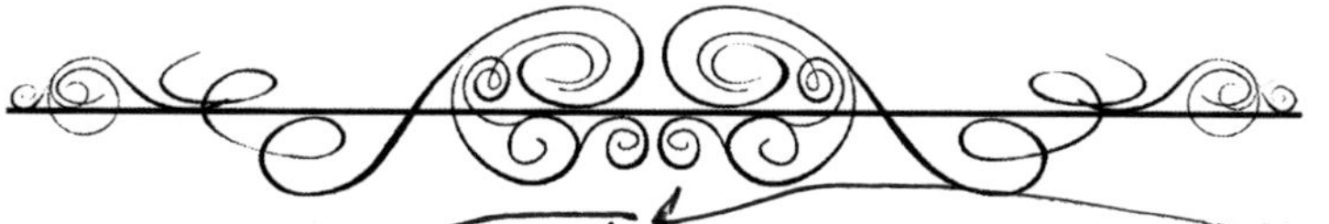

too-holy name, the title *Adonai* is the most often used substitution for Yud-Hay-Vav-Hay. In the Old Testament, the Tetragrammaton is found as the capitalized word "LORD."

Most non-Jews believe that the best translation of God's revered name is *Jehovah*. Jehovah first appeared as a result of the 1278 A.D. work of a Spanish Monk named Raymundus Martini. In a Latin document titled *Pugio Fidei*, Dagger of Faith. Martini mixed the vowels from the title Adonai with the Tetragrammaton and arrived at Jehovah. From there it was used in other works until it was used for the first time in 1530 by Tyndale in an English Bible.

Although this English name of God, or Lord, is NOT considered the "true" name as it is an English transliteration of a Hebrew name that is itself without vowels, Orthodox Jews will omit the vowel and write it as G-d, or L-rd, still recognizing it derives from the sacred name of God. God's many names are in the Hebrew Bible, Talmud, and Jewish liturgy. They are understood to reveal to man the different characteristics that God has shown to His people throughout their history.

Like Adonai, HaShem is a very popular name for God and means just that, "The Name." In Leah's life as Jacob's wife, HaShem is the name of God who responds to Leah's circumstances and blesses her with children. We read that HaShem heard Leah's prayers or that HaShem knew that Leah was unloved. We also read that Leah talks of HaShem's response to her prayers and so she names her children accordingly: Reuben, because HaShem had seen her affliction; Simeon, because HaShem had heard that she was unloved; Levi, because she hoped HaShem would join her husband to her; Judah, because she would praise HaShem.

El-Shaddai is the Almighty God who invited Abram, "*Walk in my presence and be blameless. Between you and me I will establish my covenant, and I will multiply you exceedingly.*" Using this name, which literally means "All Sufficient," God makes it clear to Abram that whatever he is being asked to do, he will do it with the might of the one who is "all sufficient" behind him. There will be no need to

worry, there will be no need for fear. Even in the midst of circumstances that may seem foreboding, El-Shaddai promised to be at Abram's side.

When El-Shaddai, the Almighty God, provides Abram with a heroic rescue of Lot, it is Melchizedek who proclaims that this Almighty God is, in fact, Jehovah-Elyon. Thus revealing another aspect of God's character as the *Lord Most High.* The emphasis is on *most high* as it was often the case that pagan nations pitted their god against an enemy god and whoever had the most powerful, or most high, god was the "winner." In using the name Jehovah-Elyon, there is no mistake that in these daily battles of "whose god is better," the God that Abram serves is the Lord Most High, sovereign Creator and Ruler of the universe, bar none.

When questioned by Isaac as to the whereabouts of the ram needed for sacrifice on Mount Moriah, Abraham's confident response was to use God's name Jehovah-Jireh, meaning "God will provide." As Christians we can understand this in that God has provided His Son as a sacrifice for our sakes. He is our Jehovah-Jireh, our God who provides a way to Himself and a means for our salvation.

In choosing to reveal characteristics of Himself through different names at different times in the Torah, God helps illuminate His nature in a way that, although we can never fully comprehend or completely define who He is, we can better understand that He has a rightful place in every aspect of our lives; in the minutia and in the grand scheme of things.

He is our healer (Jehovah-Repheka) and the Lord of Hosts (Jehovah-Tsebaoth). He is always there (Jehovah-Shamah) and is righteous (El-Tsaddik). He has perfect knowledge of all things and as Christians we call Him omniscient while our Jewish roots use the name El-De'ot. Just as we would hope, He is compassionate (El-Rachum), gracious (El-Channun), and strong (El-Sali).

And we are blessed to call Him Father.

## Good Deeds

*The word mitzvah, writ large and uttered reverently, means an act which I perform because God requires it of me. ~Rabbi Arthur Lelyveld*

Central to Jewish theology is the understanding that man is made in the image of God (Genesis 1:27) and that God calls His people to be holy, just as He is holy (Lev. 19). In this call, God has given His people 613 mitzvahs, or commandments, to perform; 248 of them are deemed positive and include such things as studying and teaching Torah and sanctifying God's name while 365 are considered negative and include such things as not to worship idols and not to practice sorcery.

In a world filled with countless opportunities to easily stray from one's path towards God, these mitzvahs provide a clear and concise guide to living. At the heart of following these commandments is one's relationship with God; itself the focus of the first six positive commandments:

1. Believing in God
2. Unity of God
3. Loving God
4. Fearing God
5. Worshiping God
6. Cleaving to God

Throughout the ages, the term "mitzvah" has taken on a broader meaning and has come to include a general attitude of performing good deeds for others. But regardless of how the term continues to evolve, at the core of Jewish life are these acts performed out of love for God. As Catholic Christians, our lives, too, reflect our understanding that how we live and what we do while we are alive, are the clearest messages we send to others. When we follow the Spiritual and Corporal Works of Mercy, we, too, are responding to God's interest in our daily lives.

**The Seven Spiritual Works of Mercy**

1. To convert the sinner
2. To instruct the ignorant
3. To counsel the doubtful
4. To comfort the sorrowful
5. To bear wrongs patiently
6. To forgive injuries
7. To pray for the living and the dead

**The Seven Corporal Works of Mercy**

1. To feed the hungry
2. To give drink to the thirsty
3. To clothe the naked
4. To give welcome to strangers
5. To visit the sick
6. To visit the imprisoned
7. To bury the dead

What we find when we give fuller attention to these works of mercy is that our own lives, interestingly but not coincidentally, become more meaningful. Just ask anyone who has offered their time to a local nursing home or has helped at a charity event (this doesn't include all the ones we do for our children's schools!). And what is most remarkable is that the works of mercy we perform in which no one can repay us tend to be the most rewarding. This is why burying the dead is considered such a "mitzvah" in the Jewish faith. This is an act of kindness that cannot be repaid.

In man's truest relationship with his Creator it would be impossible NOT to perform good works because these works would be performed out of pure love. In this way there would be no other motive, no ulterior interest in anything other than pleasing God. These works, then, are not the rote works condemned by Paul but are, indeed, the natural expression of a love for God so penetrating in one's heart that the carrying out of them would be impossible to restrain. And while we are completely aware that we are not

justified by these actions performed in the flesh, they bear witness to our understanding of Jesus' warning: *"Not everyone who says to me 'Lord, Lord' will enter the kingdom of heaven, but only he who does the will of my Father in heaven."* Matthew 7:21

When our love of God is in its truest form, in those fleeting moments of our lives when we are **completely** in union with Him, it would actually be painful not to serve Him through our works. That space deep within ourselves created for His own indwelling would feel so cavernous that it would become a physical pain, like an addiction, that could only be satiated through good works of the flesh. And even then, truly like an addiction, we would be spurred on to do more and more; each work drawing us closer to Him and creating an even deeper desire to serve Him.

When we appear before the judgment seat and receive good or evil according to what we have done in the body (2 Corinthians 5:10), it is because Christ knows, as witnessed by His own sacrifice at the cross, that real, true, unadulterated faith and love always results in real, true, unadulterated action. As we prepare for the second coming of Christ it is always important to ask God to provide us with opportunities to perform mitzvahs for His glory, for His kingdom, done out of our love for Him.

## *Intercession*

According to the teachings of the Jewish faith, the lives of the Matriarchs and Patriarchs had many purposes. There were immediate, earthly goals that each accomplished for God and His kingdom and there were generational, eternal goals that each accomplished as well.

Most people are familiar with the ways in which the Matriarchs (Sarah, Rebekah, Rachel, and Leah) and Patriarchs (Abraham, Isaac, Jacob, and Joseph) set the stage from which the three monotheistic faiths emerged. However, few people are aware of the ways in which these same Matriarchs and Patriarchs are understood to have created the "connections" between God in heaven and His people on

earth below. Indeed, delving into the teachings of the Jewish faith we find that these same people who forged a relationship with the one, true God while on earth are also the same people who became, based upon their calling, the first heavenly "intercessors" with specific areas of "expertise."

It is in the exegesis of Torah that the ways in which the Matriarchs and Patriarchs opened up the heavens for us are made known. A Catholic can easily identify the importance of such supporting documents of the Torah—i.e. Talmud, Mishnah, and various authoritative rabbinical writings—when he or she recognizes our own faith's reliance on such critical works as *The Catechism of the Catholic Church.* Additionally, documents such as *Humanae Vitae* and *Mulieris Dignitatem* and so many of the other great works of our popes enlighten and enrich our faith. Indeed, these writings reflect papal efforts to clarify Scripture and to make known the ways in which God's Word is to be understood and followed. When we read such scholarly works we more clearly see how the teachings of our faith—and choosing to follow them or not—ultimately impacts our lives.

Torah describes Abraham's circumcision and healing in the heat of the day where, even in the midst of his own pain, he cared for travelling strangers who appeared at his tent. It is then extrapolated and taught by rabbinic scholars that Abraham became the intercessor for the times in our lives when we need to exhibit more mercy, kindness, and generosity towards others.

Likewise, Sarah was known to have been a great convertor of her pagan neighbors to the monotheistic faith of Judaism. In that way she served God while on earth but also became an intercessor for the times in our lives when we are called to bear witness to God. Sarah can be called upon to help us gain strength and courage in situations where being a witness is neither easy nor popular because she was given the same strength and courage in similar circumstances. Sarah would also be an intercessor for a woman who is trying to get pregnant as Sarah, herself, experienced many years of being barren.

Catholics have always had a great reliance on the angels and saints. The *Catechism* teaches that intercession can and should be an integral part of our daily lives. The Lord has given us great resources in the way in which saints have special gifts that help us in our earthly journey. *CCC* 2683 states:

*The witnesses who have preceded us into the kingdom, especially those whom the Church recognizes as saints, share in the living tradition of prayer by the example of their lives, the transmission of their writings, and their prayer today. They contemplate God, praise him and constantly care for those whom they have left on earth. When they entered into the joy of their Master, they were "put in charge of many things." Their intercession is their most exalted service to God's plan. We can and should ask them to intercede for us and for the whole world.*

The Virgin Mother, one of our most cherished intercessors, would have known the teachings of her Jewish faith and may well have called upon the intercession of the Matriarchs and Patriarchs to give her strength as her heart was pierced, just as Simeon had foretold. When we, as Catholics, ask Mary to "*pray for us now and at the hour of our death*" we are asking for the intercession of our Jewish mother whose own faith would have given her the same sort of intercessory love, strength, and compassion that she now gives.

Relying on the intercession of Mary—and the great cloud of witnesses—is beautifully and theologically rooted in the Jewish faith.

## *Feminism*

When John Paul II wrote *Mulieris Dignitatem*, he opened with the Second Vatican Council's closing message. In his own way, JPII used that powerful verbiage to set the stage for a much needed understanding of where women stood, both in the Church and as women of God and followers of Christ.

*The hour is coming, in fact has come, when the vocation of women is being acknowledged in its fullness, the hour in which women acquire in the world an influence, an effect and a power never hitherto achieved. That is why, at this moment when the human race is undergoing so deep a transformation, women imbued with a spirit of the Gospel can do so much to aid humanity in not falling.*

At the time of JPII's writing, in 1988, feminism had become quite "radical." Women were floundering to understand who they were and in their "identity" quest, mistakenly believed that they ought to "masculinize" themselves. What began, years before, as an attempt to right some of the wrongs inflicted upon women, the feminist movement began inflicting their own wrongs upon the female population. The pendulum had swung from one extreme to another with the result still being one in which women were victims. Only now the culprit was other women.

John Paul II knew it was both necessary and important to share with his flock—males and females—what God had intended when He created man and woman. Throughout the *Mulieris Dignitatem* discourse, JPII brilliantly sheds light upon the phrase "equal but different." The reader of *Mulieris Dignitatem*, whether man or woman, cannot help but see the error in not living each and every individual life in accordance with God's plan. And make no mistake about it; God has a plan for every child—even aborted children—as well as every human person in all stages of life and death. John Paul II spends a great deal of time expounding on the gift of "self," which is ultimately the way in which a woman creates with God but is also the way in which she serves God through the love and care she gives to others.

Another important point that John Paul II spends time on in this profound writing is God's punishment in the words, "*Yet your urge shall be for your husband, and he shall be your master.*" These words were not meant only as a punishment for women, but also a punishment for men. Men were not created to rule and wield power over women but were intended to share in their divine appointment in marriage and in life. Man and woman were created with each

bringing a unique and necessary piece to the home, the family, the community, and the world. When man misinterprets these words from God, man is losing out just as much as woman is and thus the punishment is complete for both.

Woman "urges" after her husband not in a physical sense but in the longing for the husband's role or position. Thus, feminists have effectively portrayed to the world the great pain of a woman who disregards the need and necessity of a man being a man and a woman being a woman. This isn't to say that each has gender specific roles; but, rather, each individual has a vocation from God that ought to be filled (think Queen Esther or Judge Deborah or Sarah or Rebekah). A woman may indeed be called to be president and a man may indeed be called to support that woman—what is important is that a woman does not reject her inherent gifts as a female because in rejecting these gifts from the Creator is rejecting the Creator Himself and His plans for her; plans which are always meant for her good, her growth, and her eternal reward.

What is far more important than pigeon-holing male/female roles is that each is responding to the marriage union in a mutually respectful and loving way. When God calls a man or a woman, God calls the spouse as well. This truth is seen again and again in Scripture. Consider Noah's wife. Could Noah's mission be accomplished without the Mrs.? No. Each was equal, but different, in the roles necessary for the saving of mankind during the flood.

But what does this really mean: equal but different? And what is the harm in aspiring to being politically correct and thus seeing everyone as the same? Our answers are found in the Matriarchs of the Jewish faith: Sarah, Rebekah, Rachel, and Leah, the original feminists.

Four specific adjectives are applicable to Sarah, the first Matriarch, and to whom God's promise of an heir to Abraham clearly resides. Sarah is referred to a beautiful, prophetic, regal, and barren. In the politically correct world of feminism at least two and probably three of these adjectives would be considered objectionable. Certainly we

have been led to believe that it isn't appropriate to call a woman "beautiful" and yet isn't it true that some women are more attractive than others? Do we deny that God has made us different in our appearances?

Whether we agree or disagree with such a label, Sarah was a physically beautiful woman. This particular attribute paved the way for Abraham to gain passage through Egypt and made her attractive enough to Pharaoh so that he would "want" her and yet in the "wanting" of her be punished by God and thus we find Pharaoh heaping material goods and possessions upon Abraham. Yes, Sarah's physical beauty served God's purpose. She never used it to her own benefit, or coyly; but she was simply a beautiful woman who served God.

There is a perfect, divine plan in which the complementary relationship of male and female can offer balance to a woman whose physical attributes—or even emotional temperament—could otherwise lead to destructive behavior. In recognizing original sin as the foundation of lustful thoughts and behaviors, it can be understood how physical beauty can be seen as a gift from God or how it can be a source of objectification and abuse. In either situation, what it depends upon is the mutual respect and understanding of how man and woman are meant to be in union with one another.

Additionally, it is important to point out that when Scripture identifies a woman as physically beautiful—particularly in the Old Testament—it is often an indicator of her interior beauty as well. Other words that could be used to describe Sarah would have been virtuous, honest, righteous, and trustworthy.

Along with being beautiful, Sarah was considered prophetic. Just as Catholics have a mystical aspect of their faith, so, too, do God's Chosen People. In this way, Sarah was said to be prophetic in that she spent a great deal of her life converting her pagan neighbors to the monotheistic faith of Judaism. She "understood" the things of God, just as JPII speaks of in *Mulieris Dignitatem*. JPII specifically

says, "*Christ speaks to women of the things of God and they understand; there is a true resonance...*"

Thus, a true feminist embraces and values her prophetic nature, that ability to "understand" the things of God. It is only in the "understanding" that she is able to work with God, that she is able to be who God has called her to be. Sarah was in a powerful position and used that position as God intended it to be used but was only able to do so because of her spiritual nature, because she worked in union with Abraham. When feminism abhors a woman's innate ability to "know the things of God," radical feminism is asking a woman to masculinize herself and "turn off" that part of herself that God created for His own indwelling. A true feminist may attain great heights of notoriety and fame or may never be known but joyfully lives the vocation to which God has called her live.

Sarah was also said to be "regal." This would have been applicable to the way she physically carried herself as well as the way in which she carried herself through difficult times. In that way, her regality was tied to her barrenness. It was within the midst of her great personal despair of remaining childless that she witnessed to her own personal commitment to the one true God. As much as others may have attempted to provoke Sarah and question the ***real*** power of the God she served, Sarah remained regal in her ways. After all, to outsiders, Sarah was professing the power of a God who wasn't giving her children; but Sarah wouldn't be dissuaded. This isn't to say she was without fault and it can easily be said that in her own jealousy or impatience she took matters into her own hands in asking Abraham to take Hagar as a surrogate; but, in this way God is able to assure us, today, that He will remain faithful to His promises even if we make mistakes and have lapses in judgment.

Sarah is followed by Rebekah who, herself, is a mighty and formidable Matriarch, a real feminist who "understood the things of God." It is said that the divine presence that left Sarah's tent upon her death, returned when Isaac married Rebekah. The Holy Spirit was with Rebekah, just as the Holy Spirit is with each woman today. Our Advocate and Ally, the Holy Spirit allows us to discern and live the vocation to which God has called each of us. Not only are we equal but different to men, the Matriarchs remind us that we are equal but different from one another.

As feminists try to erode all labels they ask that each of us strive to be equal to—and the same as—the men they despise; but also that we be equal and the same to one another. On the other hand, Catholic women who feel faithful to Church teachings also ought to be cautious in their own views. One acquaintance recently told me of her own prejudices when she rallied against any woman coming to "power." This woman shared with me that she could now see the errors in her own attitudes because they were simply at the opposite ends of the radical feminist spectrum. A view can't be applied in a one size fits all way but must be applied in a way in which each person is supported in his or her own vocation, to which God has placed upon him or her.

JPII writes about spousal love and commitment in such a way as to make us understand that in the married state, when God calls one, He is also calling the other. Thus, the joining of a Christian man and a Christian woman in the Sacrament of Marriage is not merely a symbol of unity but is a real and actual union on which God ought to be able to rely. It is in His presence that a couple proclaims their love and support of one another, and the ways in which each may be called to serve God.

Rachel and Leah are the Matriarchs referred to in the blessing given to Boaz for his marriage to Ruth. It is the union of Boaz and Ruth that gives us the lineage from which Christ will be born. Rachel and Leah, and their two maidservants Zilpah and Bilhah, bring 12 boys into the world from which the 12 tribes of Israel will derive. So when, generations later, in the town of Bethlehem, Boaz marries Ruth, Boaz's elders say, "*May the Lord make this wife come into your house like Rachel and Leah, who between them build up the house of Israel. May you do well and win fame in Bethlehem.*"

Credit for the building up of the house of Israel is clearly given to two women, feminist in that they fulfilled their vocations as given by

God and not by man. These were women who pursued the idea of motherhood and did not consider it a burden to bear children. In fact it was a joy to co-create with God and to help build His kingdom on earth. The very idea of purposely removing a child from a womb would have been abhorrent to these women of God.

Feminism, then, must be defined as a woman filling her vocation—a vocation to physical motherhood, spiritual motherhood, and/or serving the community—with and through her own unique feminine genius. In this way true feminism has roots that reach back thousands of years and is packed with myriad examples of women called to a wide variety of vocations with no two being alike but all serving God and following His edicts.

Defining feminism by secular standards only causes continued pain, confusion, and frustration being heaped upon women today because feminists aren't quite sure they recognize feminism when they see it. "Feminists" refuse to admit that a man and woman existing is a mutually loving and respectful union is the ultimate feminist statement because in such a relationship each will uplift the other.

Thus, a **true** feminist recognizes and embraces the gifts she has uniquely been given by God as "woman" and understands that her inherent worth exists because she has been created with love by her heavenly Father; she does not wish to negate the differences between male and female but more readily pursues them as valuable to her journey on earth and necessary in God's plan.

Consequently, a feminist may be a woman like Noah's Wife who has remained forever anonymous but whose work on the ark would have been critical to its success. A feminist may be a woman like Queen Esther who was given a role of prominence and fame and who filled it with the humility of one who understands that all things come from God. Feminists are our own daughters who will fill vocations as homemakers or teachers or spiritual mothers or presidents as each is created with an equal dignity that comes from God but whose vocations may be as different as night and day.

*Dalet-Ayin-Tav,* means "to know." It is the basis of a sexual relationship between and man and woman as prescribed in the Torah. *Dalet-Ayin-Tav* is not just the physical aspects of the marital relationship; but, as John Paul II points out in *Theology of the Body*, it is the giving of self that involves a depth of personal and mutual commitment and responsibility of one spouse to another. It is meant for marriage and can only be achieved, as God intended, in marriage.

The Torah teaches that the physical aspect of the marital union, which JPII refers to as "nuptial," is really a reflection of the ultimate male-female Love that exists within the union. So, while the sexual urge is something that can and does exist whether or not a person is married, it is not intended to be an end in and of itself. It, this "urge," is what will allow a husband and a wife to "know" one another in an exclusive way. Their knowing of one another is expected to extend beyond the physical knowing and well into the emotional knowing in such a way that this intimacy brings about the "whole" person. This is the becoming "one flesh" in Genesis 2:24.

Acknowledging the potentially destructive physical "urges" to which man (male and female) may succumb, Jewish law teaches the need for self-control in these matters. Indeed, Jewish teachings on modesty and chastity are very much at the root of Catholicism's teachings on the same subjects. So while the libido can take on one form in which it will propel a man and a woman to the greater union of marriage, setting up house, and building a family together; that same libido can be the destruction of whole civilizations when pursued for its own sake—think Sodom and Gomorrah.

Maimonides, a great 12th century Jewish sage, writes: "*No prohibition in all the Torah is as difficult to keep as that of forbidden unions and illicit sexual relations.*" An argument could easily be made that Christianity's puritanical views of human sexuality were

promulgated more as a way to help man overcome this urge and not condemn himself to eternal damnation than anything else.

Consider the fact that a recovering alcoholic must forbid himself from even one drink lest he binge; so, too, could man be unable to reign himself in once he gives in to his urges outside of their original intentions. Sadly, our current society seems to have given in to those urges. Are we not seeing the consequences of immoral and highly suspect behavior in all walks of life? As a new definition of marriage is being sought around the country, and already embraced around the world, will we see the final destruction of our country as it falls into moral decay?

The Catholic Church has long taught that the home was the first and foremost cornerstone of a society. This is very much rooted in the teachings of Judaism in which the first marriage of Adam and Eve is meant to become a role model for man, until the end of time. Yes, even the deceptions that took place within that first marriage are meant to shed light on how highly susceptible we are to one another within our marriage. The influential power that exists within a home must be acknowledged. Again, that home being mirrored in society. A home that has fallen in upon itself will be seen in a society that will eventually do the same.

Throughout *Theology of the Body*, JPII brings in the first book of Torah—Genesis—because it is the very foundation upon which man's relationship with, and meager understanding of, his Creator must begin. It is in Torah that man understands his vocation of, and in, marriage. Jewish law has always taught that it was evil to pursue sex for personal gratification. Hence, the pursuit of sexual relations outside of marriage is wrong. In fact, it is deemed wrong and sinful. Marriage has been set up in Torah as the way in which a man and a woman become complete and most mirror God's plan for humankind.

Can we see the connection between pursuing sex outside of marriage, for personal gain and gratification, as perpetuating the objectification of women? Of course we can. Do we see the

connection between the birth control pill, and the subsequent "sex" for "sex's" sake as contributing to the objectification of women? Of course we do. How ironic that the very passionate claims that such things as sexual freedom and "control" over reproduction were necessary for the liberation of women have instead led to the very serious degradation of women. This is what our beloved Church has always tried to make clear in its teachings and writings about marriage and home and family; the family is sacred and reproduction a sacred right.

Jewish teaching considers having a family the way in which one freely participates with God in creation. Indeed, it is considered the most selfless act that a two people can participate in, when they have children. And rightly so because whether it is in biological form, adoptive form, or in spiritual form, being a parent is a demanding and all-consuming role. A selfish person opts out to pursue his or her own desires while a selfless person makes a commitment to become a parent (in any of the ways mentioned).

In writing *Theology of the Body*, John Paul II brought it all home, so to speak. He was making a bold statement that it wasn't just what God "wants" but it is about what God wants *for us.* Reading *Theology of the Body*, we can confidently say that God wants us to enjoy ourselves within our marriage and that joy comes from the physical and emotional connection that can only come from within that union. This is Jewish teaching at its very core.

When JPII speaks of unity as existing in "communion of persons," he is revealing that man was a solitary being until woman made him complete and whole. Together, they share a physical intimacy that transcends the physical and becomes an emotional and spiritual union as well. Without it, man is incomplete, he is alone. With it, he is completed; he is no longer alone as he now exists in "communion" with another. This other is to whom he is able to give all of himself. Jewish teaching speaks of the "mitzvah," or good deed, of a man satisfying his wife. There are many levels to this, just as JPII speaks about the many levels of intimacy that exist in the union of a man and a woman. In other words, sex within marriage

is anointed and a blessing to both spouses while sex outside of marriage is nothing more than an evil act of self-gratification, a giving in to urges in which man is actually behaving no more different than an animal.

Since marriage is the foundation upon which the whole of society can be built, the same can be said in that it reflects the ability of two to make a personal commitment to one another that mirrors their ability to make a commitment to Christ, who is at the center of this Sacrament. The logic would be this: If you cannot maintain a commitment to someone who you see on a daily basis, someone to whom you have made an earthly covenant with; how will you ever be able to maintain a commitment to God, who you cannot see, but to whom you have made a heavenly covenant?

Entering a marriage provides an opportunity to experience the earthly joys that are possible within it, as identified in the "two shall become one," while also providing an opportunity to witness to an eternal expression of self. Adultery, then, is not just a moral indiscretion but a sin against Christ. Jesus is, after all, at the center of the union. JPII calls adultery a "sin of the body" while also using the vivid imagery of an "adulterous" Israel breaking its covenant with the one true God when it becomes like its pagan neighbors.

When the Catholic Church teaches of the inherent good that comes from the family unit, the pleasures that come from the physical union of a husband and a wife, and the covenantal implications of adulterous behavior, the Catholic Church is shepherding her people in the way Christ intended. When John Paul II wrote the individual components of *Theology of the Body*, he revealed to us, his flock, the ways in which God calls us to into communion with Himself and with one another in marriage.

## *Mysticism*

Human history shows that man has always sought a connection with God that transcends his mere day-to-day experiences. Man wants to know God intimately, deeply, privately—to fill that place within his heart which God created for His own indwelling. St. Augustine perfectly captured this earthly feeling when he said, *"Our hearts are restless until they rest with Thee."* Indeed, Augustine's life (354-386), as told in his *Confessions*, beautifully reflects the ways in which man experiences earthly restlessness and pursues Divine intimacy.

Jewish mysticism, which dates back to the beginning of the Common Era, has always been a response to that personal quest. Along the way, it is known to have flourished during different times including—in northern Spain—in the twelfth century where, it is interesting to note, St. Teresa of Avila would eventually experience her own inner mystical conversion in the 1500s and ultimately become, in 1970, the first female doctor of the Church.

The study and practice of Jewish mysticism—known to be uniquely powerful—was originally forbidden unless a Jewish male was at least 40 years old. This was considered an age where he would have had enough years of Torah study upon which to be firmly grounded in faith since mysticism has both the potential for the development of good as well as the unleashing of evil.

The Catholic Church affirms this dual possibility of mysticism and approaches the subject of mysticism with caution. She warns against pseudo-mystics as well as the formation of doctrines, such as pantheism, in which false teachings are perpetuated under the guise of mysticism. To safeguard against such corruptions, the Church relies upon the works of such Catholic mystics as Teresa of Avila and John of the Cross to help guide the faithful through the different phases towards Divine union.

This paradox of exposing oneself to good or evil in spiritual practices is easy to understand when you consider the many horrors that have occurred, in our lifetime and in the history of civilization, in the name of "God." This has the potential to happen when ego, if not put fully aside, becomes empowered in selfish and delusional ways. In St. Teresa's writings on her mystical experiences, her humble attitude towards self is ever-apparent. Early Jewish rabbis

would have clearly understood that human ego has a way of polluting the heart. What is meant for our good can bring us harm.

Sadly, mysticism today is often misunderstood and has recently been linked with new-age thinkers as a result of the revelation that Madonna (the pop icon and not the Blessed Mother) practices teachings from the Kabbalah, one of the earlier known works on Jewish mysticism.

Kabbalah (which literally means "tradition" but connotes a "handing down of tradition"), is a school of thought in regards to contemplative prayer and union with God. Studying Elijah was a central point of early Jewish mystics. Reference to the "Chamber" experience appears in Jewish mysticism long before St. Teresa of Avila's own experience, as shared in *Interior Castles.*

St. Teresa of Avila and St. John of the Cross embarked upon their mystical journeys in the 16th century. And as Kabbalah had its beginnings in Spain a few hundred years before the lives of both of these Catholic mystics, there has always been speculation of a connection between those mystical teachings and the spiritual journeys of Teresa of Avila and St. John of the Cross.

Certainly, St. Augustine's own 4th century journey, literally and figuratively, speaks volumes about man's interest to heed God's call for intimacy in the ways brought about by contemplative prayer and the practice of mysticism.

It is always imperative to remember that St. Teresa of Avila called humility "truth," recognizing it as the required approach for such a transforming spiritual experience: Galatians 2:20, "*I have been crucified with Christ. It is now no longer I that live, but Christ lives in me.*"

Does this mean, however, that all who attempt or pursue the mystical experiences of Augustine, Teresa of Avila and St. John of the Cross are successful? No, it doesn't. In fact, the Catholic Church specifically recognizes that while it is a natural desire for man to

search for such a connection with the Divine, the graces needed to accomplish this are given to just a few souls. That being said, the idea that it is both a possibility, and a desirable one at that, makes us search out the meaning of mysticism in our daily lives.

So what is mysticism, really?

Simply put, mysticism is the soul's desire to be in union with God; it is the contemplative practice in which this goal can be attained. For most of us, the journey towards that experience is life-long and while often unfilled (to the degree in which such Saints as Teresa experienced union with God which is called "spiritual marriage"), it is still satisfying. That is because God rewards those who persevere and there are a great many joys inherent in the pursuit.

The day-to-day practice of contemplative prayer creates a peaceful existence for one's soul. It is the constant giving of self, and the giving over of one's will to the will of God, that will bear spiritual fruit. Contemplative prayer, of which the *Catechism of the Catholic Church* says is an "intense" time of prayer (2714), the "simplest expression of the mystery of prayer" (2713) and a "gaze of faith, fixed on Jesus" (2715) is the form of prayer used by mystics—modern day and those in our Church's history.

Catholics have always understood that the earthy passage "matters" and that salvation, given through the grace and mercy of God through His Son, *can* be lost (Romans 2:2-8, Ephesians 2:8-10, James 2:14-26). Just so, the development of the soul does not occur on its own but does so with a daily commitment to prayer and the pursuit of intimacy with the Creator. Certainly we can also agree that the conscience cannot rightly form on its own. All these things (maintaining, or keeping, the gift of salvation as well as development of the soul and conscience) require an "effort" on our part. The *Catechism* states that while we may not always be able to spend time in meditation, we are always able to enter into the inner prayer of contemplation (2710).

Throughout Church history—from Pope Gregory I to Blessed Henry Suso and beyond—Catholic mystics have given examples of ways in which our soul's longing to connect with God can be fulfilled. Contemplative prayer, and the ways of the mystics before us, are just a few of the tools we are able to use in answering our call to know, love and serve God in this life and be happy with Him in the next (Baltimore Catechism).

## *Oral Law*

When HaShem (God) dictated the Torah to Moses, that Written Law, or Torah She'bi-khetav, made God's laws known to His people. This Truth, in all its glorious revelation, was to provide the Jewish people with instructions for daily living, how to celebrate their holidays, and the ways in which they should worship their Creator. The Torah is also unambiguous on the behaviors that should be avoided and gives clear directions for atonement of sins committed. Although the Written Law was considered complete, traditional Jewish teaching is that Moses also received a second set of laws called Torah She'bi-al peh: the Oral Law.

Accompanying the Written Law, the Oral Law gave the finer details on how the Written Law was to be fulfilled. For instance, work was forbidden on the Sabbath but the people needed to know, more specifically, what constituted "work." Thus, the need for the Oral Law. This Oral Law, then, was given to Moses who gave it to Joshua. Joshua, then, told the Elders and the Elders then told the Prophets. This transmission took place during the First Temple Era and spanned the approximate years of 950 to 586 B.C.

By the time of the prophet Ezra, around 490 B.C. in the early second temple era, a group of Levites would be at the side of the scribe and priest giving an oral interpretation to what was being read from Torah She'bi-khetav. It was also during this time of the Great Assembly that the Oral Law was collected and eventually, with the destruction of the second temple, put into an outline form known as the Mishnah. The Mishnah was completed in 188 A.D. and was meant to provide a means for students of the Torah She'bi-khetav to better remember the Holy Book. With time the need for more in-depth analysis of the Mishnah grew and resulted in a work of explanations called Gemara. Together, the Gemara and the Mishnah make up what is called the Talmud.

Catholics, too, have always believed that the Bible is the word of God, and, like the Chosen People, Catholics have relied on other sources to deepen their understanding of Scripture, knowing full well that nothing could ever add to Scripture or detract from Scripture but only shed light upon it. We, as Catholics, believe and trust in the Holy Spirit to guide us, individually and collectively, in knowing God fully through His word. Indeed, the Church, being guided by the Spirit, existed before the New Testament and had to rely on the oral transmission of the life of Christ before the Holy Spirit guided different people to record these accounts. And then, again, the Holy Spirit was relied upon to gather and determine which works would become the New Testament.

Catholics believe that the Holy Spirit has been at work in the development of both the New Testament and in its teaching. Like our Jewish ancestors, we recognize that God, through His Spirit, deems certain people more capable of this task than others. This isn't to say that the average lay Catholic does not have an informed opinion about Scripture but that we look to the Magisterium as the final authority. We do, we should, and we do well to diligently study Scripture.

In the early years of the Church, local communities were each led by a bishop whose job it was to give a faithful, Spirit-led transmission of Christ's life and His work. Along with passing on the faith, Bishops were expected to defend it and work towards the unity that Christ intended. Today, lay Catholics continue to delve into the Word of God, learning and exploring the holy writings that intimately connect us to our Creator. But Catholics also recognize the role that the Pope and Bishops play in edifying, for us, the Word of God. We are blessed to turn to papal encyclicals, the *Catechism*, and numerous letters and documents that cover a vast array of topics from abortion to family matters to work to war. Just like the

Jewish people turn to the Talmud to deepen their understanding of Torah, we turn to these sources with the same intention. Believing that Christ did not leave us bereft, we have trusted in the Spirit's guidance of our Magisterium and will continue to do so in the millennia ahead as we eagerly await His return.

## *The Immaculate Conception*

From the time of Abraham's response to God's call to leave the country of his kinsmen, God began the process of preparing the way for the Messiah. Abraham, after all, introduced to his pagan neighbors the objective truth of the one God; Creator of all that is, was and ever shall be. He was being set aside for this intention. Along with his wife, Sarah, Abraham is credited throughout Jewish teaching for converting pagan neighbors to the monotheistic faith of Judaism. Abraham, being set aside for that purpose, was able to remain a vessel for God's plan.

Not only was Abraham a vessel for God; but Abraham acted as an intercessor as well. Consider his dialogue with God, in which God is prepared to pour out His wrath and punishment upon Sodom and Gomorrah. Abraham beseeches God to withhold punishment if Abraham is able to find but a small handful of citizens who have not succumbed to the moral decay of their neighbors. God enters into this dialogue because of Abraham's faithfulness and the faith in which Abraham has lived his own life, following God.

The evolution of God's plan, which began in earnest with Abraham's visible commitment to monotheism, continued throughout salvation history. People, and even items, were often set aside, to be used in this plan for man's deliverance. Q*adosh* is the Hebrew word that means set aside, or separated, for a purpose. Throughout the Old Testament people and things had often been set aside for specific purposes. When God called upon Israel to be a people like no other and to be a kingdom of priests, those priests were "set aside" for specific duties. Utensils, vessels, and garb that were meant for service at the altar of the temple were "set apart" and would not to be implemented elsewhere, less they would be defiled. So this

"setting aside" was a common understanding of the Jewish people. Abraham was "set aside" when he was asked to leave his homeland and the evolution of being set aside was underway.

When Mary is called the "Immaculate Conception" she is simply reflecting two thousand years of Jewish practice in which something meant for God's use, for His salvific plan, is set aside. It is not a new teaching but, rather, rests upon Jewish laws that are thousands of years old. And, just as the priests, utensils, and garb were set aside, Mary, too, was set aside and thus the "Immaculate Conception." Additionally, just as these things—whether people or items—acted as intercessors between God and His people, so, too does Mary act as intercessor as well. This is the culmination of thousands of years of preparation for the Messiah that began with Abraham's being called from his homeland. Mary, then, as the one who would offer her human body to be the vessel for Christ, would have had to have been put aside, as taught for the two thousand years prior to her saying "Yes."

## *Silence*

Abraham instructed his servant to leave Canaan, return to Abraham's homeland and find a wife for Isaac. Abraham was far too old to make the journey himself and trusted in God to make the search for a daughter-in-law a successful one. Abraham's servant, likewise, trusted in this same God. The servant set out to Abraham's homeland mirroring the same belief that God would be part of the journey and reveal the woman who was meant to become Isaac's wife.

Very early in Scripture we see that a relationship with God has many facets. It involves trust, diligence, faith, and silence. Securing Rebekah as Isaac's wife, and thus the woman to whom God's promises would continue to manifest, began with trust. Abraham trusted that God would provide the wife who was intended to carry on the mantle of Sarah. Abraham's servant, making an oath, also had this same trust. Abraham's witness over the course of his lifetime, in fact, brought many of his pagan neighbors to an understanding of the one true God and thus earned him great favor

in the sight of the Almighty. It was, undoubtedly, this act of witnessing that allowed his servant to travel on such a journey with the confidence that one ought to have when journeying with God.

But what begins with trust, however, must also involve diligence. Walking with God does not translate into a life of, as they say, leisure and bon-bons. Rebekah didn't come waltzing into town and announce she was from Abraham's homeland and thus show herself as the one who was intended to become Abraham's daughter-in-law. No, Abraham had to turn his trust in God into action that reflected the trust. It required him to become involved in such a way that God could act through Abraham's actions; actions that, as we see in Genesis, required using an outside party, namely Abraham's servant.

Indeed, trusting in God turns us into His instrument because we become aware of the greatness of His plan and the need to surrender in such a way so as to become, literally, that mechanism. Here, the instrument is Abraham's servant who takes on the same attitude of trust and then diligently proceeds, with the implementation of God's plan, to secure a wife for Isaac. Notice how telling it is that Abraham had to rely on someone else even though God's great promise had been made to Abraham. Again, early in Scripture, we see the roots of our faith that calls us to community. The Jewish roots of who we are as Catholics is evidenced by this reliance on another person to help us in our journey with God.

So, we begin with God's plan for Abraham's descendants to be more numerous than the stars in the sky. God both reveals and promises this to Abraham. Abraham must display trust in such a way that he (Abraham) can move forward with this belief and become actively involved in the plan. Remember, though, that Sarah made the rash decision to hurry this plan along and had given Hagar to Abraham which resulted in the birth of Ishmael. And while God promised Hagar that Ishmael would become the father of many, this still wasn't the original intention of God's revelation to Abraham. Thus we see that God's promises were not made only to Abraham but to the coveted marriage of Abraham and Sarah. Once again our Jewish

roots reveal to us, as Catholics, that the sacredness of the sacrament of marriage, and God's view of us "as one," began with Adam and Eve and is reiterated with Abraham and Sarah.

We also see the real notion that our time is not God's time, that even when we understand God's plan, we ought to be aware of the delicate balance between waiting for it and working towards it.

This is where Abraham's servant reveals to us the critical piece of working with God: silence. *The man watched her the whole time, silently waiting to learn whether or not the Lord had made his errand successful (Genesis 24:21).* Silence is an act of faith in our earthly journeys. Its timing is an integral component of a successful walk with God. Like Abraham, his servant, and Sarah, we all have a decent amount of trust in God. And, like these same people, we all have a fair amount of energy to persevere for His kingdom.

So it is fitting that a simple sentence in the story of Abraham, Isaac, and Rebekah makes a point of telling of the necessity for silence. A time where discernment can take place and, in this story, where the servant can be made aware of God's "answer." Consider the reality that the servant was embarking on a journey that was anointed by God and yet he (the servant) did not presuppose his own will over that of the Creator's. He (the servant) continued to turn to God with each step of the journey to get his bearings, so to speak.

That time of silence is often where we may find ourselves squirming because we are anxious to hear from Him. We are ready for answers and feel that we've been fruitful enough to warrant them. And the idea of silence may make us even more fretful when we begin contemplating that the answer we may hear could be "no." Abraham's servant, however, was willing to hear just that. We can assume he was exhausted from his journey (just as we may be) and maybe he would have felt a bit broken in spirit if Rebekah was not "the one" and yet, in faith, the servant waited to hear her offer of water. Those would be the telling words that God had said "yes."

The servant wasn't testing God but earnestly attempting to carry out His will. The servant was showing us that while we set out in trust and then actively participate with diligence, we ought to be mindful of the importance of waiting, in silence, to hear from God. With faith we know that God's response to our questions will be right, timely, and true. Catholics often speak of discernment and Abraham's servant shows the value of waiting and praying—keeping silent so that God may respond and we will hear.

Jesus had many demands on His time. People sought Him for healing and counsel. He was busier than any of us could ever imagine. And in the midst of His busy walk on earth, He showed us the need for silence. Christ would separate Himself from the daily tasks of His life as Lord and Savior and seek silence with His Father. We often say that He took on human form to experience life in such a way as to be able to empathetically relate to our own experiences. He became our example for resisting temptation, to live with a humble spirit, and to show how to should serve one another. He, too, became our example of the need for silence. Jesus shows how it is often in this silence that God is able to soothe our aching heart and share answers to our prayers.

## *Work and Worship*

'Avodah' is the Hebrew word that means both "work" and "worship." Whether in Genesis where God put man to "work" or in Exodus when God instructs Moses to approach Pharaoh with the request to release the Hebrew slaves so that they can "worship" God, the word 'avodah' is used. The image of both work and worship are powerfully integrated by this dual use of avodah. Used interchangeably we are to see that God can be honored with our work. John Paul II understood this innate way in which work and worship were tied together when he wrote his encyclical, Laborem Exercens.

*Work is a good thing for man-a good thing for his humanity-because through work man not only transforms nature, adapting it to his own needs, but he also achieves fulfillment as a human being and indeed, in a sense, becomes "more of a human being." ~ John Paul II, Laborem Exercens; September 14, 1981.*

That John Paul II would put forth the point that in work we achieve fulfillment indicates that it is in our working that we become fully alive, as God intends! Laborem Exercens is replete with John Paul's insightful understanding of avodah. He makes it abundantly clear that through our daily lives, regardless of what it is we "do," when joined with Christ and offered to God, work is what makes us "more of a human being." Indeed, it is our work that John Paul II identifies as separating us from other creatures.

Early in Genesis we are called to subdue the earth; and although the word "subdue" may have somewhat of a negative connotation in a politically correct world, it is nonetheless a direct instruction from our Creator. As such, there is no reason to believe that "subdue" is anything other than God's way of showing that, in the scheme of things, we are "at the top." This shouldn't offend or frighten us but should help us realize the great responsibility we have as workers during our earthly sojourn. Christ shows us in washing the feet of His disciples that we are called to serve one another and in this service are working for God's kingdom.

We should rejoice that we have been given that dictate and pursue the ways in which we can honor God through our daily activities: our work. As JP II eloquently points out, every human being, throughout the generations and even into our current technological existence, is part of the process of subduing the earth.

Additionally, the Catechism identifies work as a duty and states that everyone should make legitimate use of his talents to contribute to the abundance that will benefit all; and every worker should be allowed to harvest the just fruits of his labor (*CCC* 2429). As Catholics we are called to embrace ways in which our talents can benefit our family and our community. In doing this we are practicing avodah in that our work is also a way in which we worship our Creator—by using the gifts He has given us and by showing our obedience to His word. We often believe, mistakenly, that witnessing is the act by which we subtly, or non-so-subtly, bring our faith into our conversations. Or, unsure of our own abilities, we often forgo witnessing altogether. But avodah says that working diligently, honestly, and with integrity, wherever that may be, is a way to worship and witness as well.

## *Set Aside*

*Therefore, gird up the loins of your mind, live soberly, and set your hopes completely on the grace to be brought to you at the revelation of Jesus Christ. Like obedient children, do not act in compliance with the desires of your former ignorance but, as He who called you is holy, be holy yourselves in every aspect of your conduct, for it is written, "Be holy because I am holy."* ~ 1 Peter 1:13-16

"*With the passage of time, holiness does not lose its force of attraction; more than that, it shines with greater luminosity.*" John Paul II wrote these words about St. Seraphim of Montegranaro (1540-1604). They are similar to words that John Paul II wrote, years earlier, about Josemaria Escriva, a priest and the founder of Opus Dei, and Josephine Bakhita, a Daughter of Charity of Canossa. Those of us blessed to have lived a significant part of our adult lives with John Paul II as pope have come to know him as a man of great personal commitment to the Gospel, to evangelization, and to making us aware of what he often called, "The universal call to holiness."

The Hebrew word for holy is *qadosh* and while it has a number of derivatives, this is the word that the Lord used when He revealed His own holiness and our call to follow. In this case, the word *qadosh* means set aside, or separated, for a purpose. We can and should assume that, as Christians, we have been set aside for His purpose. Throughout the Old Testament people and things had often been set aside for specific purposes. When God called upon Israel to be a people like no other and to be a kingdom of priests, those priests were "set aside" for specific duties. Utensils, vessels, and garb that were meant for service at the altar of the temple were "set apart" and would not to be implemented elsewhere, less they would be

defiled. So this "setting aside" was a common understanding of the Jewish people.

As *qadosh* originates in the Old Testament, it is then crystallized in the New Testament when St. Peter encourages an evangelized population to continue moving forward with hope in their newly baptized lives and in the resurrection promises. Specifically, St. Peter refers to **conduct** as being deemed "holy." He recognized the draw of the secular world and of falling prey to its ways, often our own "old" ways. St. Peter knew the ease with which we could succumb to the world, thus forgetting that we are "set apart for God's purpose." St. Peter's letter (although some scholars attribute authorship to a disciple of St. Peter's) is at once both chastising and yet a call to holiness. There can be no coincidence that our own John Paul II, himself a successor to the seat of St. Peter, would continue to caution and yet inspire us to the "universal call to holiness;" to a clearer understanding of how we are to conduct ourselves in our daily lives having been set apart for God's purpose.

When we understand the true nature of the Lord's call upon us to be set aside for His purpose we also understand how we are to use His graces towards that end. 2 Corinthians 9:8 says, *"Moreover, God is able to make every grace abundant for you, so that in all things, always having all you need, you may have an abundance for every good work."* So it is only right to ask ourselves how we have responded to this centuries old call initiated by God and brought to man through the seat of St. Peter. Are our lives evident that we have been set apart for God's purpose? Is it clear to anyone looking on that we are "different" than our surroundings? Catholics are over a billion strong. A billion! When a billion people respond to a call to holiness, the world literally becomes a different place.

## *Feast of Tabernacles*

*All who are left of all the nations that came against Jerusalem shall come up year after year to worship the King, the Lord of hosts, and to celebrate the feast of Booths.* Zechariah 14:16

Autumn has always been my favorite season. I absolutely love the cooler temperatures that bring crisp night breezes wafting through the open windows and the beauty of leaves changing colors on all the trees. College fight songs, stores filled with back-to-school supplies, and wardrobes that include warm and fuzzy flannels are harbingers of the peaceful days that will fill the season. I'm not yet waylaid by inches of snow and slush nor am I suffering through the humidity of the dog days of summer. Yes, in my heart, there is no other season that holds the magic of fall.

Autumn also ushers in the last of the fall harvests, the final crops. Farmers Markets are filled with the best of the fruits and vegetables from the season and there is a smile on everyone's face as they peruse the succulent choices for purchase. It is no wonder that this time of year is of special importance to our Creator, as well. It is during this time that Sukkot, the feast of Booths, is celebrated.

*The fifteenth day of this seventh month is the Lord's feast of Booths which shall continue for seven days.* Leviticus 23:34

The equivalent of this fifteenth day of the seventh month changes each year but is always joyful. It has been said that to have seen it celebrated during Christ's time is to have seen joy beyond comprehending. And it is no wonder that during this blissful time Jesus revealed Himself as the fulfillment of this pilgrim festival that calls everyone in Israel to celebrate at the temple.

At the core of the Sukkot celebration is the Sukkah itself. This is the booth, or tabernacle, that each family makes, according to specific guidelines. Essentially, both building the booth and dwelling in it for the seven days, or some portion thereof (see Lev. 23:42) is considered a mitzvah, or good deed. The booth is supposed to have only one permanent side and its roof is to be made of something grown from the ground but not tied together as it sits upon the tabernacle. In a spiritual sense, the temporary structure reflects our own temporary existence and ultimate dependence on God. The roof, while providing some protection, should allow the occupants to gaze up into the stars at night thus being able to know and

worship God more intimately. And of course, the entire structure harkens to the 40 years that the Jews wandered the desert, depending completely upon God for food and shelter.

Sukkot is on the heels of Yom Kippur, a time of fasting and atonement; the most solemn of occasions on the Jewish calendar. It is fitting that Christ would deliver such clear words about Himself and His ministry during this pilgrim feast because Christ is, for us, both atonement and then joy. It is His blood that covers our sins and thus allows us to follow Him, the first fruits of death, to a joyful resurrection.

*On the last and greatest day of the feast, Jesus stood up and exclaimed, "Let anyone who thirsts come to me and drink. Whoever believes in me, as Scripture says: 'Rivers of living water will flow from within him.'"* John 7:37-38

Sukkot ends with a celebration called Shemini Atzeret or the Ceremony of Water Drawing. Also marking the beginning of the rainy season, Shemini Atzeret is a day devoted to the love of God and honoring His interest in spending time alone with His people (Num 29:35). For seven days visitors, neighbors, and friends have gathered in happiness and joy. Now the guests have gone home and Adonai holds His people dear to His heart for one more day; a special time together. The Torah readings come to completion and readings begin anew showing that God's word is never-ending; just as our earthly life will come to its end, only to be renewed in an eternal life.

Water, so rich in meaning, here can be seen as the pre-figurement of the Holy Spirit being poured upon God's people at Pentecost as foretold in Joel 3:1 *Then afterward I will pour out my spirit upon all mankind.* During the Ceremony of Water Drawing the Levitical priest would use a special pitcher with which to draw water from the pool of Siloam; where Christ had cured the blind man. Shofars would sound and the water would be poured on the great altar. It is during this time that Christ reveals Himself as the giver of living baptismal waters—the sender of the Paraclete, the redeemer of men.

The Illumination of the Temple is yet another significant part of Sukkot. During the Illumination of the Temple, candles are lit and bring such light that nothing is said to be left in the dark. So when Christ says in John 8:12, "*I am the light of the world. Whoever follows me will not walk in darkness, but will have the light of life,*" He is revealing that He is able to, like the illumination of the temple, bring a light that has no end; in His light, nothing remains in darkness. He lights the way to the Father and also sheds light upon our sins. It is in this illumination that we are called to respond, to repent, to seek refuge in His atoning death.

*And the Word became flesh and made his dwelling among us, and we saw his glory, the glory as of the Father's only Son, full of grace and truth.* John 1:14

Jesus Christ is the fulfillment of all that the Feast of Tabernacles promises. He is our Sukkah, our shelter; He is our water, our salvific baptismal water; He is our light, our illuminated path to the Father. Sukkot, also known as the Feast of Booths, the Feast of Tabernacles, and the Feast of Ingathering makes God's plan completely known to man. In all ways Christ is truly the fulfillment as He has tabernacled Himself among us and has provided us with a safe haven for our eternal life. Of all holidays that the Lord calls His people to celebrate, this Feast of Ingathering is the most significant because it says to us Gentiles, that we, too, belong to Him. When Christ makes His return to gather the final harvest, we will find that we, too, are His fruit.

# *Role Models*
# *for*
# *Today's Catholic Women*

## *Women in Your Faith History*

*In the "unity of the two," man and woman are called from the beginning not only to exist "side by side" or "together," but they are also called to exist mutually "one for the other."*

Mulieris Dignitatem

## *A Woman's Worth*

From Eve to Sarah to Deborah to Mary, Scripture assures every woman who has ever lived that her life is both special and valuable. Her life has a purpose and a meaning set by God and necessary to His plan for humankind. Each and every one of us came here with an extraordinary set of gifts and a particular set of circumstances. Our births were the intentional acts of an affectionate, devoted God whose love for us is truly immeasurable. We are as unique and varied as the stars in the sky. Our gifts and talents are limitless—even if they sometimes feel non-existent or without value.

The seasons of our lives, our experiences, and our dreams are a thing of beauty and honor. We may lead or we may follow. Some of us will feel exhilarated while others of us will feel exhausted. And then the experiences reverse. And those whose time it is to reap will reap while those whose time it is to sow will sow. We share more than a common faith heritage with the women of the Bible. Yesterday, today, and tomorrow we remain the same in that our life has an anointed meaning and a distinct purpose.

We may lose sight of this reality in all our "busy-ness" but it, our precious life, never loses a meaning and purpose set by God. It is true that it all passes by in the blink of an eye but that is exactly why God shares the stories of the women in our faith history. He wants to let us know that we are valuable and unique with gifts that are meant for our joy and His glory. We are all equally loved by God. Oftentimes we may look at another's circumstances and think, "Gee, God must love her more than He loves me. She sure seems blessed!"

However, nothing could be further from the truth. We simply do not know the details of each other's journey and the virtues God may be attempting to develop or experiences that God is allowing for our own good.

Like a parent who marvels at her ability to love each of her children so fully, so completely, so it is with God's love for us. Each and every one of us enjoys His full and complete love. He is enamored with us, one and all. It is that deep and abiding love He has for us that bring opportunities for us to develop virtuous behaviors or learn valuable lessons. The life that God has given each of us is really a uniquely packaged gift meant to bring eternal reward.

So, as we embark on our pilgrimage, searching for Truth, Scripture calls us to look deep into the lives of the women whose stories are told. Scripture beckons us, knowing that we can be touched by His precious words, His beloved heroines.

In Scripture we see courageous women, warrior women, and women rulers. Some women in Scripture have been embraced while others have been cast out. Women have brought both evil and salvation. Women, the Word of God shows us, are the embodiment of strength and ability in some of the most vulnerable of situations. They can save or destroy nations. Their fortitude is awe-inspiring. While teaching us about their own lives we find that they teach us about our lives as well.

Women of Scripture speak to us in familiar and loving ways. They know our struggles and reach to us in their stories. They help us learn how to live a life pleasing to God and yet fulfilling for ourselves. We find assurance that our own uniqueness is both expected and nurtured. In studying and understanding Scripture we come to see that these women, these role models, all have their own special relationship with God. Some women have had the audacity to be in disobedience to God while others are in complete obedience. Some argue and chortle at God while others revere His existence. In the end, each and every woman's relationship with God is

wonderfully her own. In this way, no woman today is left without a heroine—regardless of her life's circumstances. Whether she is homemaker or warrior, her predecessor is in Scripture. We see silent women, joyful women, powerful women, repentant women, and wily women.

Through it all we continue to be assured that each and every woman whose mention appears in a verse, a paragraph, a chapter, or a book is there for a reason. Her story might be our story. Her story might be our best friend's story or our sister's story. Her story exists for a reason just as she existed for a reason—just as each of us exists for a reason. For His reason we came into being and for His reason we move forward into the world. We, too, are courageous women and warrior women and women rulers. We, too, are silent women, joyful women, repentant women, and wily women.

John Paul II wrote about "Feminine Genius." Feminine Genius is a woman's unique gift from God which allows her to most effectively live her life and serve God. A woman is most fulfilled by cultivating her gifts and understanding her inherent worth and dignity. John Paul II spent a great deal of time and effort ensuring that women understood the fundamentals of being created in the image and likeness of God. John Paul II was very intent on making sure that women were not displaced in their roles as wives, mothers, caregivers and friends through what is often seen and understood as a radical feminist agenda of gender-neutrality. One would have to assume that JPII's immense interest in helping women embrace their inherent dignity arose from the degradation he saw as society continued to pit women against women and the ways in which sexual freedom and "reproductive" rights put women in a more vulnerable, more objectified position than ever before.

John Paul II knew that every day women rise to the challenges before them, become "gifts of self" to others, and are meant to draw strength from the knowledge that with God they be truly fulfilled and fulfilling.

The fact remains: if we fail to do our job, or reach our destiny, we leave a hole in God's plan. It is imperative that we understand that no one can do what each of us is uniquely called to do. We are different for a reason: His reason.

Embracing the Word of God, examining the lives of women in Scripture, allows us to embrace our own individuality. So, whether it is in our home, in our relationships, at work, or in some distant corner of the world, our purpose is ours alone. An opportunity to be most fully alive is found in achieving that purpose.

In sharing with us His anointed examples of the women in our faith history, God shares with us His understanding of our struggles and His support of us in our journey. He reminds us how uniquely He made us. He comforts us through our pain and cheers us through our successes. And while He does not promise us a life without distress, He does give us His word that He will be with us during distressing times. When we learn the ways of our Creator we find that nothing else is able to empower us like that knowledge. We are special to God and He uses the Old and New Testament alike to embrace us and to nurture us as no earthly being could. He is our God, our Creator, and our Redeemer. He speaks to us in Scripture. His Word is our answer, regardless of the question. And it all began with our creation in Genesis 1:26-27.

*Then God said: "Let us make man in our image, after our likeness. Let them have dominion over the fish of the sea, the birds of the air, and the cattle, and over all the wild animals and all the creatures that crawl on the ground." God created man in his image; in the divine image he created him; male and female he created them.*

In this beautiful telling of the creation of man and woman we hear God speaking, we hear Him formulating plans for our existence. When I read this creation verse I am reminded of the Jewish mystics who claim that a woman is born with inherent gifts to connect to her Creator and a man must "work" at attaining those same gifts. For instance, a Jewish man has far more rituals than a Jewish

woman—in fact a Jewish woman has beautiful, mystical rituals like ushering in the Sabbath through the lighting of candles; while a Jewish man is bound by law to pray three times a day and follow other, more formal edicts. Furthermore, Jewish sages say that a man is supposed to marry so that he can have what we now call "feminine genius" in his home. It is to a man's benefit to be married to a woman who understands her God-given gifts.

So this takes us back to the creation verse. Applying the Jewish mystical "take" on things, it would seem to support that God did not want to leave man alone because woman was necessary to bring the Divine more intimately into man's life. While the secular world seems intent to misinterpret these verses and call woman "an after-thought" or "second-best" the reality is that her existence was necessary for man to fully know, love and serve God. Indeed, we could no more separate a woman's role from a man's role in humanity than we could separate the Father from the Son or the Spirit. Likewise, man offers balance to woman's existence as well. They truly do complete one another.

When we are in union with Christ-like men or in friendships with Christ-like women or working with Christ-minded co-workers we find our worth unquestioned. As Christians we are also called to be those exact same things to others; Christ-like spouses, Christ-like peers and co-workers, and Christ-like friends. We are all valued and respected as co-creations of God and have an obligation to bring that realization to one another. To receive this truth we must also give this truth to others. Our life, then, is filled with reason and purpose. Our journey is blessed and anointed as we take on the task of bringing God's love and light to others through our compassion, joy, kindness, patience, and perseverance.

However, living in a secular world has taken us off our intended path. And in so doing has minimized our inherent worth in Christ who so believed in our intrinsic value that He willingly died for us. We sometimes find our life's purpose in direct opposition to our worldly existence. We are often receiving mixed opinions and are

reluctantly following advice that changes from day to day. It is no wonder that people are flocking, in droves, to anyone who has a viable message of love and happiness. God created us to be both receivers and deliverers of His love. It is part of our nature to seek out love because our original source of that love is God Himself.

But in our pursuit of that fulfillment we ought to be wary of words that are not in compliance with Scripture and His ways. This is why time spent studying the Word is invaluable. We come to know Him through the Bible and because His word is "living" we are able to see how applicable it is to us, today. Many women today are turning, or returning, to their Creator for His vision of their lives. We are relishing our own feminine genius and our roles as daughter of the King; we are—or certainly should be—inspiring one another and understand the roles women played during Jesus' time on earth and throughout church history.

Indeed, women today are yearning to carry on the tradition handed to them by their sisters-in-faith. We are finding a renewed sense of self as we embrace the wisdom found in the Scripture. In turning back to God's Word, as our source of insight and guidance, we find the support we crave. In Scripture we find heroines of every shape, size, and color. We find ourselves encouraged as only God can: with love, kindness, and understanding. We find the reason for our being. From Scripture, we can rest assured that our worth, in God's eyes, is no less (and no more) than man's.

Our society has gone myriad ways in regards to women's roles and women's rights but not so with Scripture. It was said quickly, and early on, that a woman's worth was sacred. A woman is held in the highest esteem in God's eyes. Her work is both necessary and sacred to God's plan for the world. It is a message that we should humbly acknowledge. Genesis 2:20b-23 adds another dimension to the creation of woman that is just as profound as Genesis 1:26-27.

*But for Adam no suitable helper was found. So the Lord God caused the man to fall into a deep sleep; and while he was sleeping, he took one of the man's ribs and closed up the place with flesh. Then the Lord God made a woman from the rib he had taken out of the man, and he brought her to the man. The man said, "This is now bone of my bones and flesh of my flesh, she shall be called 'woman,' for she was taken out of man."*

Without woman, man was incomplete. God's plans for humanity could not yet be accomplished. Just as the Father is only complete with the Son and with the Spirit, man is only complete with woman. When John Paul II begins his 1995 *Letter to Women* with a word of "thanks" to every woman, he is recognizing this completeness that woman brings to man and to mankind.

There was much to fill man's world and yet the need for the creation of woman was evident. It was woman, and nothing else, who would complete man's existence or more pointedly, complete God's plan. They were to work together to build God's kingdom on earth. Ultimately these verses should impress upon us our intrinsic worth. They ring peacefully in our ears and rest softly in our hearts. They are the food of our infant daughters and the nourishment of our sisters and friends. When we raise our daughters in this understanding and remind our friends of their inherent worth in Christ, we give them an awareness that can forever impact their existence.

To fall prey to the secular lies of worth as having been created "second" are to fall prey, once again, to the great deceiver. In many ways, radical feminism today seems to have taken over where the serpent left off; in presenting themselves as "liberator" and "maintainer" of women's rights, radical feminists reduced women, more than ever before, to objectification and worthlessness. This has happened because a woman can never be a man, no matter how much she is encouraged to pursue that goal, and all the while, in making attempts to be something she is not, a woman does not get to be who she is!

One of my favorite authors on the subject of "Womanhood" is Alice von Hildebrand whose book *The Privilege of Being a Woman* completely captures who we are as the "weaker" sex and demolishes the arguments about our creation as an "after-thought" that makes us second best. She bravely encourages us to recognize who we are as the weaker sex while identifying "weaker" as something that should be valued and welcomed. What is wrong, she makes us wonder, with being "fragile, delicate, breakable, vulnerable and sensitive?"

Her work specifically asks: *How many blunders do we make because we act impulsively and overlook our weaknesses and limitations?* This is an excellent and very valid question. I am reminded that as a parent I encourage my sons to honestly evaluate their strengths and weaknesses—it would be absurd to say that they are without both—and thus to be aware of and ultimately, God willing, master them by virtuous behaviors and choices. Why would that same thinking not be applicable to me, as a woman?

When von Hildebrand states, "*As a matter of fact, to be reminded of one's weakness is, from a supernatural point of view, a grace,*" we understand the damage that an agenda of gender-neutrality can have on a woman, a man and on society as a whole. It is in often only in our weakness that we learn of our utter dependence upon God and are able to walk humbly with Him. When we pound our fists upon our chests and say "*I am woman hear me roar*" we mistakenly believe in our own power and forget that all we have comes from God above. "*To be conscious of one's weaknesses and to trust in God's help is the way to authentic strength and victory,*" says von Hildebrand.

Women are uniquely gifted, as are men, and to make the claim that there is essentially no difference between the two is most ridiculous. The longings that a woman feels, because she does feel her emotions most deeply, can only be filled by God and in pursuing His plan for her life—which will include being in right relationship with "male." In other words, understanding her gifts and inherent worth and how they are meant for her own journey are squashed when she follows another path, other than her own female path. In undermining or dissolving the complementary relationships that men and women are meant to have will most assuredly have consequences beyond our imaginings.

When we encourage one another to recognize and satisfy our longing for God with God Himself, we allow each other to be free from misplaced priorities. Being free from misplaced priorities allows us to embrace our lives with revived hope and joy. Jesus left us with peace and it is in that peace we are able to live most abundantly. There is great and lasting comfort in knowing how vital we are to God's plan for the world. We need to be free from worldly messages that take us off our path to God. We will see from the women of Scripture that God's plan cannot unfold without each and every one of us. Our life was a purposeful gift from God. What we do with our lives is a gift we give back to Him.

Each woman in Scripture has a beautifully unique story that should open our eyes and our hearts to the variety of roles that we will play in our lives. Each woman catapults us into our own feminine genius in exhilarating ways! If we have allowed ourselves to be truly blessed, our earthly friendships will also reflect this diversity of other daughters of the King. We will have friends who are feisty and friends that are complacent. We will know women who are outspoken and courageous as well as women who are withdrawn and content (which is often a courageous statement in and of itself!). They are all a part of our lives, as we are of theirs, to bring completion and wholeness. We should inspire one another, console one another, and support one another regardless of our individual journeys.

Sadly, we often find ourselves at great odds with each other. We have been polarized in ways that are an affront to the God who calls upon us to love one another. We are jealous and envious when we should be supportive and enthusiastic. Working mothers find themselves in opposition to stay-at-home mothers. Mothers who

choose public schools have been pitted against mothers who choose to home-school. Women who support themselves are pitted against women who are supported by their husbands. Women who marry have been put at odds with women who stay single. The list seems to grow with each passing year.

In our quest for Truth, let us be running to the Word of God as our reliable source of guidance and wisdom. Let us measure all we hear, all we read, and all we see against the Truth of Scripture; for it alone provides the fullness that we seek. Jesus, we know, is the Truth that sets us free. Christ, as John Paul II notes, is the great ally of women. Contrary to secular messages that attempt to portray the Church and her teachings as dismissive towards women we find in the Church's rich documents the ways in which Christ uplifted women and the ways in which women served Christ most selflessly.

Consequently, we should be drawn to those people who direct us to our Creator, our source of life, and His word. All else falls short. More than ever before the often used phrase that heeds us to look out for a wolf in sheep's clothing seems appropriate.

We should, as Christian women, purposely replace the secularly accepted, new-age words like "universal being" and "ultimate power" with the correct reference to God. We, then, start to become the witnesses that Jesus expects us to be. When we remind ourselves that, upon His resurrection, Jesus first appeared to a woman, we are also reminded of His call on our life to be His witnesses. We then become instruments that God is able to use in a meaningful way. When we strengthen our love of one another and ourselves (of course in a non-narcissistic way) we are more fully participating in God's unique plan for our life and the abundant grace that He gives us to bring His plan to fruition.

When we draw our understanding and wisdom from Scripture we will find that there is a plan for the likes of each and every one of us, in every phase of our life. We will all find the heroines that God has provided in His word. We will recognize that different seasons of

our life require these different heroines, each with their own unique characteristics and personality.

In that way, Scripture becomes our lifeblood. In his *Letter to Women*, John Paul II addresses what he calls the "essential issue of the dignity and rights of women as seen in the light of the word of God." This is because Scripture connects each of us to God through all the times in our life. In God's Word we will see our friends and we will see our neighbors. We will see that we are created as loving beings that should bolster one another. We will cherish the great diversity that exists in the paths of our lives. Scripture will show us what is truly important and help us set our ways in accordance with God's mandates. Scripture will kindly show us our struggles are not new. Through God's Word we will find women that are just like us: women on a journey.

*Above all, love each other deeply, because love covers over a multitude of sins. Offer hospitality to one another without grumbling. Each one should use whatever gift he has received to serve others, faithfully administering God's grace in its various forms.* 1 Peter 4:8-10

*For the grace of God that brings salvation has appeared to all men. It teaches us to say "No" to ungodliness and worldly passions, and to live self-controlled, upright and godly lives in this present age, while we wait for the blessed hope-the glorious appearing of our great God and Savior, Jesus Christ, who gave himself for us to redeem us from all wickedness and to purify for himself a people that are his very own, eager to do what is good. Titus 2:11-14*

*And we know that in all things God works for the good of those who love him, who have been called according to his purpose. Romans 8:28*

*For anyone who does not love his brother, whom he has seen, cannot love God, whom he has not seen. And he has given us this command: Whoever loves God must also love his brother. 1 John 4:20-21*

*Nobody should seek his own good, but the good of others. 1 Corinthians 10:24*

*For this God is our God for ever and ever; he will be our guide even to the end. Psalm 48:14*

*Commit to the Lord whatever you do, and your plans will succeed. Proverbs 16:3*

*The Lord bless you and keep you! The Lord let his face shine upon you, and be gracious to you! The Lord look upon you kindly and give you peace! Numbers 6:24-26*

*Being a person in the image and likeness of God thus also involves existing in a relationship, in relation to the other "I." This is a prelude to the definitive self-revelation of the Triune God: a living unity in the communion of the Father, Son and Holy Spirit.*

Mulieris Dignitatem

## *The Holy Spirit*

Before we can even begin to look at all the interesting and wonderful women of Scripture, we must first look at our relationship with the Holy Spirit. The Holy Spirit connects the created to the Creator in the most intimate of ways. Women, when moved by the Spirit, are powerful forces. They become fully equipped to do the work of God with both His blessing and His anointing.

Unfortunately, we have been programmed to tune out all the messages and intuitions and hunches that would otherwise fill our being. Intuitions and messages and hunches that would allow our lives to be filled with graces and abound in blessings. We have tuned out, turned off, and generally abandoned a beautiful way that the Lord has always chosen to work with us. A gift that has always been ours has been sullied and ridiculed by so many people that we have found it easier to walk away.

Many of us have allowed the secular world to dominate our existence and in so doing have filled our lives with what appears to be more but is actually less: less hope, less faith, less fulfillment, and less integrity. In following today's example of "busy-ness" many of us have abandoned our spiritual selves for our secular selves.

Indeed, our everyday lives are filled with more things to do and less time in which to do them. We are encouraged to eat on the run, feed

our children on the run, and in general be "on-the-run." And with this new way of life, this new "busy-ness," we are less inclined to follow the Spirit when the Spirit moves us. We are less likely to hear the Spirit when He calls. We brush aside those inclinations in our attempt to accomplish 25 hours worth of "life" in a 24-hour day.

And there is no end in sight; women are becoming addicted to the Internet, blogs, and such social networking sites as Facebook at much higher rates than men! Women follow other women's "tweets" on Twitter, read their blogs, and in all ways have become less connected to God as they become more connected in the high tech world provided by the Internet. While Pope Benedict XVI encourages Catholic women to use the Internet as a means of witnessing and evangelizing, Catholic women should be cautious and need to honestly ask themselves if their computer time really isn't just a "wolf in sheep's clothing." We are easily able to assure ourselves that this time is providing new avenues for witnessing but are we really just deluding ourselves? Women have to take stock of their time so that Internet time it isn't being exchanged for time that will truly allow each of us to cultivate our relationship with God.

If we are not aware and cautious with our time, we quickly succumb to the world around us. The inclinations that are meant to move us through the world will no longer guide us as they are forgotten and abandoned—the real consequence of time not given to God. The Internet has contributed to our loss of quiet or silent time; time meant to stop and listen to the still, small voice of God speaking to our spirit.

According to Romans 8, in living by our nature we set our minds upon our natural desires. However, when we live by the Spirit, we set our minds on what the Spirit desires. So, in becoming absorbed by, let's say, technology, our natural desires for those things of the world begin to replace and dominate our spiritual desires. In essence we unknowingly, or unwittingly, lose track of our spiritual selves. When we are caught up in the "busy-ness" of our lives we are unable, or less likely, to produce the fruits of the Spirit: the fruits by

which Christ will know us. Galatians 5:22 identifies these fruits as love, joy, peace, patience, kindness, goodness, faithfulness, gentleness and self-control.

The very characteristics that are neither embraced nor encouraged by our secular world are the only characteristics that set us apart as followers of Jesus.

In Scripture we are told to *carry each other's burdens, and in this way you will fulfill the law of Christ. (Galatians 6:2).* The mandates in Scripture quite clearly tell us how to conduct our lives. While our society often encourages us to care for ourselves and to "win at all costs," Scripture directs us to care for each other and in that way recognize that we are fulfilling the laws of Christ. When Christ said that there would always be the poor and disadvantaged among us, He was sharing His understanding of our difficulty in serving others. Most certainly this is not what He wants, but He knows that for almost all of us, this is a real struggle; to subjugate our own selves for the sake of others. And when He died for us He gave us the consummate example of serving our fellow man.

Fortunately, when we make a point to develop our spiritual selves, the Spirit will be able to guide us in priceless ways. Let me share a story about myself and Pam…

*One hot, late July afternoon I decided to take a walk around my neighborhood. The sweltering weather was made even more so by the fact that I was overdue with my second child. As I wobbled around the block, pulling my two-year-old son in a wagon, I noticed a young mother planting flowers near the front of her home. She didn't look up as I passed but continued planting her flowers.*

*I circled the block once and, as I neared my own drive, felt inclined to circle the block again. There was no real reason to do this as neither my son, nor I, was enjoying this stroll. Nonetheless I avoided walking up my driveway and continued on with a few steps that would change my life forever.*

*As I rounded the block a second time all my senses were focused on the heat, my overdue pregnancy, and my complaining son. Out of the blue I heard a sweet voice say, "You look like you could use some lemonade." Although normally quite reserved this invitation seemed to hit a chord with me and I uncharacteristically accepted the kind offer. The thought of resting my feet and letting my son out of the wagon was just what I needed.*

*As it turned out, the invitation came from that young mother who had been diligently planting her flowers. We sat, laughed at the dilemmas of young children, talked of the weather, and went our separate ways.*

*Two days later I gave birth to my second son and, to my delight and surprise, received a beautiful bowl of fruit from the lady with whom I had shared a much-needed refreshing glass of lemonade. With the fruit she also gave me a beautiful book about raising sons (she has three of them) which I have enjoyed over and over again.*

Make no mistake about it, the Spirit will move our life's circumstances, and us, in priceless ways…

*It was late July and Pam's flowers were long overdue for planting. She finally found the time to work on them and was bound and determined to get the job done. The plants needed to get into the ground if they were going to survive. If not, she would have to throw them all out.*

*As she got to work she noticed a VERY pregnant lady walking in the street. The lady was pulling a little boy in a red wagon. It was quite hot and neither of them looked like they were enjoying the walk. As they passed her driveway the Holy Spirit urged her to speak to the pregnant lady, to say "hello." She resisted the urge as the flower matter was quite pressing. She really wanted to get this job done and enjoy the garden. She didn't want to lose the flowers. And so she let the lady pass by.*

*Pam continued working industriously when she noticed the lady passing by a second time. The little boy seemed more miserable than before and the lady looked like she was going to deliver at any moment. This time the Holy Spirit was*

*quite insistent. "Speak to her!" And so she put her trowel down, looked up and said, "You look like you could use some lemonade."*

And from those inclinations, both hers to offer lemonade and mine to take a second walk around the block, God has forged a most beautiful friendship: a friendship that has lasted twenty years and several moves. It has become a friendship that now sees children graduating from college, getting married, and having children of their own. Ours has become a friendship that has grieved over the loss of family members and rejoiced at successes. It is truly a blessed friendship orchestrated by the Holy Spirit.

I share this special story to illustrate that when we allow it, the Holy Spirit will orchestrate so much in our daily lives. From our relationships to our careers to our finances, there is nothing in our lives that we need to keep from the Holy Spirit. But having gotten out of touch with our natural ability to listen to the spirit and nurture our relationship to God, we spend time spinning our wheels. We invest our energy in things that were never meant to be and on roads that we were never meant to travel. We look to a world with a one-size-fits-all belief when we are, in fact, so customized that one size could never even fit two, let alone all.

Getting caught up in our secular existence also hinders our ability to produce the fruits of the spirit. These fruits are considered love, joy, peace, patience, kindness, generosity, faithfulness, gentleness, and self-control. We will see, as we study the women of the Bible that these fruits always seem to make their presence known. And, maybe more importantly, we recognize that God continues to provide ways for each woman, along with ourselves, to manifest these fruits based upon the circumstances of life. We also see how life is filled with opportunities to make us believe that these fruits are not necessary, or to invalidate their worth. We might find ourselves, like many of the women in Scripture, more apt to feel pangs of jealousy or pride than peace and kindness. It is in these times that we are most able to call upon Christ and redeem these moments for Him and for His cross. We then, as He has said, will find our rewards to be of the

heavenly kind. When, in our darkest hour, we are able to be most like Christ, we will see that the fruits we bear are truly from the Spirit. We do not manifest them; the Spirit manifests them so that through us His kingdom is known.

When a woman frets over her identity in the secular world, she is less apt to produce the fruits that would have been more readily available to her on her own walk in life. When she finds herself in heated competition with others, she is often unable to be an instrument for God.

We all like the idea of being valuable and full of merit and regrettably buy into the erroneous notion that we are not as valuable as our "successful" counterparts, whoever they may be—it may be a corporate executive male or a female who bakes and sews like nobody's business. It might be a mother whose children all sit quietly and perfectly in Church or it may be the couple down the block who are ready to retire at thirty years old. The sad fact is, too many things are able to distract us from our own uniqueness.

By concentrating on our own unique journey we should seek and understand our own unique gifts as well as the gifts from the Holy Spirit. These gifts are different from the fruits of the Spirit but are just as necessary in our walk as Christians. Furthermore, it becomes crucial for us to understand St. Paul's message regarding all these gifts. When accepted, these gifts become the sustenance of our spiritual existence and invaluable tools to ensure the success of our life's journey and walk with Christ. And, as St. Paul writes in 1 Corinthians 12, these gifts, unless motivated by love, become useless and invalid. They were given from the Father, with great love, and are ours to share with others with the same great love. Love, of course, being a fruit of the Spirit!

The gifts from the Holy Spirit include wisdom, understanding, counsel, knowledge, fortitude, piety, and fear of the Lord. These gifts, while valuable for our earthly existence, are meant to glorify His kingdom and for the propagation of our faith and the Good

News. Additionally, these gifts allow us to achieve the relationship with God that He so very much desires.

*Wisdom* helps us know and seek God. Wisdom separates our thoughts and our actions from the foolish and the arrogant. Wisdom guides us on our journey as we understand our true ineptness without God. The Book of Wisdom has as its purpose the elevation and splendor that is the acquisition of wisdom as a human goal. God is complete wisdom and does everything in wisdom; we, then, ought to see how wonderful and valuable wisdom is and pursue it in our own lives.

In wisdom King Solomon ruled God's people, without wisdom he succumbed to the temptations of the world. Wisdom is not a once-in-a-lifetime acquisition but a lifelong expedition that has many bumps along the way.

*Understanding* allows us to use both our heart and our head. Understanding works with wisdom as we make choices and decisions that are in keeping with God's edicts. We understand the value of a life that is pleasing to God and are wise enough to make that overall choice but also wise in the day-to-day choices that make up our lives. We understand the need to use both our compassion and our intellect when we make our decisions and as such are more apt to please God.

When we seek good *counsel* we show maturity and a level headedness that is in keeping with God's ways. When we provide good *counsel* we are sharing our wisdom and understanding of God with others to help them make decisions that are based upon the Lord's edicts and ways. We are bringing glory to His kingdom on earth.

*Knowledge* is gaining information about God and using it as He would like. When we are knowledgeable we are more inclined to be in a right relationship with God and with others. When we are steeped in the Word, we are able to draw upon that knowledge in

our daily lives. When we discern through prayer, living our life according to God's commandments, and spending silent time listening to God, we are able to acquire knowledge that enriches our own relationship with God and anoints our unique earthly journeys.

*Fortitude* is the trait that allows our faith and our hope to move us through the difficult times of our lives, having the knowledge that God works all things for His good. When we succumb to circumstances that have the potential to derail us, we are wrongly letting our situation control us when we should be persevering in God's graces and mercy. We have been told in Scripture that the battle has been won; but we may find ourselves forgetting the strength we have in that ultimate win; the Resurrection! *Fortitude* helps us run the race set before us so that we make it to the finish line!

*Piety* is a beautiful reverence for our Creator. Piety allows us to be humble as we recognize His hand always in our lives. A pious attitude is never one of arrogance or judgment. Instead, a pious attitude is one of great humility as it shows our understanding and awareness of the awesome God we serve.

*Fear of the Lord* is that realization of our deep need to have God in our lives and the fear of ever separating ourselves from Him. There is nothing wrong with fear when we understand that it keeps us "in check" as it is a simple case of knowing that God is God and we are not! In coming full circle, Proverbs 1:7 identifies that fear of the Lord is the beginning of wisdom!

These gifts from the Holy Spirit (wisdom, understanding, counsel, knowledge, fortitude, piety, and fear of the Lord) are ours as followers of Christ. The same Spirit that led Christ into the wilderness is ours to lead us from this wilderness to Christ. We need to be led by the Spirit in this life if this life is to be in accordance with God's plans.

Throughout Scripture we see women working in accordance with the Spirit, bearing fruits of the Spirit, and displaying the gifts of the Spirit. We see plans unfolding and lives guided in a rich and fulfilling way. Scripture reiterates the point that each of us will have our own particular blessings: blessings as unique as we are. But while our blessings are unique and our talents are ours alone, we are all gifted in the Spirit. It is that Spirit, His Spirit, which tries to move us in ways that are both pleasing to the Lord and satisfying to our journey.

We display the Gifts of the Spirit

Wisdom, Understanding, counsel
Knowledge, Fortitude, Piety
Fear of the Lord.

We offer (act) (live) Fruits of the Spirit

Love, joy, peace
Patience, Kindness, generosity,
Faithfulness, Gentleness
Self Control

## *The Word of God*

*Now if we are children, then we are heirs-heirs of God and co-heirs with Christ, if indeed we share in his sufferings in order that we may also share in his glory. Romans 8:17*

*But God chose the foolish things of the world to shame the wise; God chose the weak things of the world to shame the strong. 1 Corinthians 1:27*

*Many women were there, watching from a distance. They had followed Jesus from Galilee to care for his needs. Matthew 27:55*

*Get Wisdom, get understanding; do not forget my words or swerve from them. Do not forsake wisdom, and she will protect you; love her, and she will watch over you. Wisdom is supreme; therefore get wisdom. Though it cost all you have, get understanding. Proverbs 4:5-7*

*May the God of hope fill you with all joy and peace as you trust in him, so that you may overflow with hope by the power of the Holy Spirit. Romans 15:13*

*The Spirit of the Lord will rest on him-the Spirit of wisdom and of understanding, the Spirit of counsel and of power, the Spirit of knowledge and of the fear of the Lord-and he will delight in the fear of the Lord. Isaiah 11:2-3*

*Now to each one the manifestation of the Spirit is given for the common good. 1 Corinthians 12:7*

*You are my friends if you do what I command you. I no longer call you slaves, because a slave does not know what his master is doing. I have called you friends, because I have told you everything I have heard from my Father. John 15:14-15*

*In the light of Revelation, creation likewise means the beginning of salvation history.*

Mulieris Dignitatem

## *Eve*

Eve was the first woman. Her very existence began as a loving effort on God's part. She completed man and was given dominion, with man, in the Garden of Eden. She walked in the Garden of Eden secure in her knowledge of God's love. Like Eve, we too exist because of God's great love for us.

Scripture tells us that God knew us before we were born. It is a telling statement of God's great love for us to imagine that He knew all about our iniquities, shortcomings, and sinful natures and yet loved us into being. If we are parents, it is very much the way we feel about our own children. Our children are able to bring us great joy and great sorrow. Given that knowledge, we would still make the same choices that brought them into our lives.

And so it is with God except He knew us BEFORE we were born. His knowledge was far deeper than ours was with our children. Women expecting their first babies often fantasize about the complete joy that their children will bring. They mark off the days on the calendar with an unparalleled eagerness. They are not counting on the arguments that lay ahead or the difficulty that will come with raising children. Their minds and hearts can only see the good.

But our benevolent Father saw so much more than that before our own births. He knew of the delight He would have in our existence but more so knew of the snarls that were ahead.

God was well aware that we would, like Eve, come into this world with a free will that would allow us to make our own conscious

choices. He knew that we would, similar to Eve, make a wide variety of decisions, some good and some bad. Nonetheless, God still willed our existence. He still welcomed our life, knowing that it would be filled with moments both pleasing to Him and moments disappointing to Him. With great anticipation, He still loved us into being.

When we question His love for us we only need to remind ourselves that He knew what our life would hold and still desired our birth. When we wonder if we could ever be worthy of His immense love, we only need to recall His forgiving nature to those who, like us, disappointed Him or put roadblocks in His path. Do we not, if we are parents, feel the same for our children?

Certainly we know of the deep disappointment that our children, or our loved ones, might bring into our life and yet wouldn't we, given the opportunity, still gladly receive them again and again? And so it is with God. He continually embraces our efforts to return to His fold. His love is greater than our most toxic transgressions. He has given us His Son so that we may forever, in claiming our salvation in Christ, be saved. Christ's death allows God's arms to be forever open to us.

Eve's story shows us that when we put our own self-interests before God's we do more harm than good. Our Father in heaven wants the best for us and has provided for all our needs. As He did for Eve, He does for us. She roamed the Garden of Eden with all her needs met. And yet, that didn't seem to be enough. Eve, in the Garden of Eden, could still be tempted. As baptized followers of Christ we will also find that temptation and sin are a very real part of life.

In the dialogue between Jesus and Satan (Matthew 4) we witness the ways in which Satan will try to draw us in and become accomplices in our own downfall. Satan says to Jesus, "*If you are the Son of God tell these stones to become bread.*" Of course Jesus is wiser and stronger than Satan's enticement and is able to respond, "*One does not live by bread alone, but by every word that comes forth from the*

*mouth of God."* Satan continues to try to tantalize Jesus but Jesus will not be worn down. In this exchange we become aware of the fact that temptation is a lifelong struggle. The world says to us, "*If you are successful you will drive 'this particular car,'*" or, "*If you are a 'somebody' you will live in 'this kind of house,'* or *"If you are a good parent your kids will have 'this particular amenity.'"* And, like Jesus, we need to be strong against these tantalizing messages: messages that confuse our priorities and take our eyes off God.

We aren't tempted only once in life. We aren't free from future temptation simply because we are able to overcome a particular allure or addiction. Temptation is a part of life and a weakness that Satan will prey upon. The Gospel of Matthew makes that clear.

Eve's experience in the Garden of Eden shows us that temptation and sin are very real things. Most certainly, we can understand the appeal of that "one thing" that is beyond our grasp. In all honesty, it would be difficult for us to say that we would have, most assuredly, made better choices than Eve. Consider our circumstances now. Do we always avoid sin and temptation? As I asked earlier, how tempting is the Internet and technology-led social networking in our lives? So, in that one moment, Eve captured our temptation with hers. She reminded us how vulnerable we can be, even in the most rewarding of circumstances. And so she sinned.

But as we know, God will always work things to His good and so He sent Jesus to conquer sin, but not our sinful nature. That is our cross to bear. And while the secular world would like us to renounce the reality of sin, our Savior requires us to acknowledge it and consequently His redemption. The socially acceptable message leads us to believe that we can redeem ourselves. We are often led to believe that we are that powerful. However, Scripture assures us that redemption comes only when we approach Christ with true repentance.

In Eve's reach for the apple she made a choice that forever changed human history. In believing the ultimate liar, she stepped out of

grace and in so doing, brought about the first sin. The consequences of her actions were immense and seemed to throw the human condition into untold turmoil: child bearing was to become painful and the earth was to become unresponsive in its yield. There would forever be enmity between the serpent and Eve's children. Life would be, as we have experienced, filled with strife. Make no mistake, God was clearly letting us know that there would be dire consequences for our sinful actions and that responsibility would always rest upon our own shoulders. Denying our culpability transcends into our own denial of the salvation that Jesus brought. Although unpleasant, and certainly contrary to popular belief, we are sinners.

We live in a world where we are encouraged to attain more, yearn for more, and set materialistic goals. This is why Jesus reminds us that we cannot worship two masters (Matthew 6:24). Indeed, we oftentimes find ourselves being very shortsighted and believe that an earthly treasure has worth. We might buy into the message that possessions will allow us to possess joy. But nothing could be further from the truth. Joy is ours for the taking when we align our lives with God's commands and dictates.

That spot in our heart that God created for His dwelling can only be filled by God Himself. We learn from Eve that, regardless of the temptation, we should never put our interests above God's Word. When we become the kind of self-centered people that are often nurtured and encouraged in our secular world our view becomes myopic. And as we lose sight of the whole picture, we most assuredly lose sight of God. Or, we begin to see God through the societal messages that deny the existence of sin and its consequences. We begin living with a shortsightedness that becomes a detriment to all that God had in mind for our lives. Our sins, we are told, are minor. Or they are insignificant. Or, more appalling, they aren't sins at all. And so we go our merry way, having forgotten that Eve is our first example of sin and its grievous consequences, especially transgressions without repentance.

We sadly forget that God sees, knows, and orchestrates the "bigger" picture while we only experience a fragment. We begin to believe in our own omnipotence and our own omniscience. We make decisions out of alignment with God's edicts and assume that the little fragment of life that we see is life in its entirety. This is the danger of the corporeal message.

It is that fragment of understanding, both in sight and in knowledge, which is too often being fed by our secular world. That segment then, becomes our guide and our focus as we take our eyes off of God and put them on the things that we begin to believe have value. Eve did just that. She took her eyes off of God and focused them on the one thing she couldn't have: something she mistakenly believed had value. And with her focus off God she was easily able to disobey Him. We, then, immediately learn from Eve how very critical it is for us to keep our focus, our undivided attention, on God and His will in our life. We see the consequences of actions that harm our relationship with Him. We see them loud and clear.

Fortunately, we also learn from Eve God's great love for us, sinners. As sinners we are able to accept the redemption that Jesus offers. If we reject the notion of our sinful nature then we ultimately reject the notion of our salvation. We cannot have one without the other. We know the end of the story. We know that God sent His Son so that we could regain our standing with Him. In Eve's story we see that we must always keep our faith in God whose love is bigger, more extensive, than our worst sins while still recognizing our sinful natures. If we accept the biased message in which our God requires little liability from us, we reject Jesus.

We must consider ourselves accountable for our sins while remembering that we serve a God who only wants the best for us. We should remain attentive to our Lord who sees the whole story when we can only see a page. In the end, God knows our struggles and assures us that He will always draw us back to Him, through the Son. God will lead us back to Him when our focus becomes blurry and our reasoning becomes faulty. When we present Him with a

repentant heart He welcomes and absolves us. He is a God of love and a God of forgiveness.

Eve's life shows us how vulnerable we are when we give in to our "weak" selves. If we deny who we are as women, then keeping guard against that part of ourselves that is more emotional—more prone to "fancy" as St. Teresa of Avila has written—then we make it near impossible to overcome our weaknesses when the time comes for us to be strong in Christ.

Once again we recognize that in our weakness we most perfectly are able to depend upon God. As Alice von Hildebrand points out, "*Both the Old and the New Testaments condemn pride, arrogance, self-assurance, and the stupidity of those who believe they do not need God.*" Eve reminds us how very much we need and ought to rely on our Creator.

Even though our destiny was altered that day in the garden, we know that Eve, like ourselves, was part of God's loving plan. She taught us how to be mindful of our free will. Eve brought God into our lives in a richer way. Because of Eve, our free will can be a true testament of our acceptance of God's will and hand in our lives. Through Eve's disobedience we are given use of our own free will in such a way that our choosing God is more pleasing and more meaningful.

The more we move through the world and encounter women from all walks of life, the more we realize that women are strong and resilient creatures. Yes, we make mistakes. But as Christian women we have the full knowledge of God's sanctifying grace in our lives. That knowledge allows us, when our hearts are burdened with sin, to repent and return to His strong arms, wiser and more able to do His will. It is through free will that both our love and repentance are so meaningful.

It is not surprising that women find themselves in situations where their true strength is so often showcased. Women, by their own

nature, bring both delicacy and force into the world. They are capable and worthy mothers, neighbors, leaders, and friends. Women are powerful, passionate, and strong. They often have great loads to bear but do so with God forever at their side.

Eve's story should always remind us of God's tremendous love for us. A love so deep that it brought the Son; His Son, who was able to, once and for all, forgive the transgressions of a remorseful human race.

In many interesting and varied ways Eve makes us take stock of ourselves. Eve makes us recognize our sinful nature and reminds us to keep God at the center of our lives. Eve enlightens us regarding our free will and the consequences of our actions. She is also a witness to the strength and capacity we have to be resilient in the most difficult of circumstances. She teaches us to be grateful and content, believing in God's anointing in our lives. Finally we learn from Eve that, regardless of our sins, God is both willing and longing to accept our penitence and embrace our return to Him.

## *The Word of God*

*Dear Friends, let us love one another, for love comes from God. Everyone who loves has been born of God and knows God, because God is love. 1 John 4:7-8*

*If you remain in me and my words remain in you, ask for whatever you want and it will be done for you. John 15:7*

*When Jesus rose early on the first day of the week, he appeared first to Mary Magdalene, out of whom he had driven seven demons. She went and told those who had been with him and who were mourning and weeping. Mark 16:9-10*

*Humility and the fear of the Lord bring wealth and honor and life. Proverbs 22:4*

*Hear, O Lord, for you are a God of mercy; and have mercy on us, who have sinned against you; for you are enthroned forever, while we are perishing forever. Baruch 3:3*

*In the Lord, however, woman is not independent of man, nor is man independent of woman. For as woman came from man, so also man is born of woman. But everything comes from God. 1 Corinthians 11:11-12*

*So God created man in his own image, in the image of God he created him; male and female he created them. Genesis 1:27*

*The Lord God said, "It is not good for the man to be alone. I will make a helper suitable for him. Genesis 2:18*

*Trust in the Lord with all your heart, on your own intelligence rely not; In all your ways be mindful of him, and he will make straight your paths. Proverbs 3:5-6*

*The Lord delights in those who fear him, who put their hope in his unfailing love. Psalm 147: 13*

*The biblical teaching taken as a whole enables us to say that predestination concerns all human persons, men and women, each and every one without exception.*

Mulieris Dignitatem

## *Noah's Wife*

Sometimes, maybe even more often than we would like, our lot in life seems to be mundane but necessary. Day after day, week after week, we clean bathrooms, attend meetings, shop for groceries, do laundry, and carpool. Our lives are so full of chores that it seems as if we could be replaced by one well-oiled robot with decent driving skills. Yet we continue on with the belief that what we do makes a difference, and rightly so!

We find gratitude in the small things, the simple "thank-you's," and the occasional hug. It is our hope that from our tedium will arise treasures. We nurture our children, tend to our sick neighbor, and comfort our co-workers. We do these things for our family, our friends, and our neighbor knowing that caring for others is an edict from God. Deep inside we know the worth of our actions and trust in the value of what we do. We have a deep and unwavering faith in God's plan for our life. Part of that faith comes from learning others' stories and seeing how God worked in their lives.

Noah's wife and daughters-in-law are the heroines for the time in our life when we have to reach deep within ourselves and find joy where others might not. From Noah's wife, and her daughters-in-law, we clearly see how God is working miracles while she is taking care of the day-to-day necessities. Like us, there must have been times that these women wanted to give up, throw in the towel, and collapse from exhaustion. But they kept on working. Not because

they were above reproach but because they were fulfilling God's purpose in their lives. God's design was energizing them just as it often energizes us. It gives us momentum when nothing else will. It is important for us to draw strength from the knowledge that our everyday lives, when truly lived for God's glory, never really have an ounce of tedium in them.

Whether we are loan officers, volunteer clinicians, restaurant workers, CEOs, or full-time mothers we can never underestimate what we bring to others in our daily living. Just as important is the realization that it is the commitment to our everyday tasks that allow us to develop the perseverance required to be Disciples of Christ. From that foundation of tenacity Christ will be able to bring our lives into fruition and blessed beyond imagination.

If we are not finding joy in our everyday lives or are unable to give gratitude for what we currently have, we cannot ask to move ahead and acquire more. It is to our benefit to work diligently, for God's glory, in whatever circumstances He has put us while we thank Him, and believe in His word, for the blessings that are unfolding. Just as Noah's wife was assiduously working to make the ark's mission a success, so were untold blessings unfolding for the future of mankind: namely its survival.

We find renewal in the understanding that, when we are working with God, our journey will be enriched by a wide variety of people and circumstances in which we are both givers and takers. We do not see what God has in store but should put our complete faith and trust in Him.

Had she known what lie ahead, what might Noah's wife's reaction have been at the outset of the journey? Like most of us, she must have seen her own weaknesses and probably would have abandoned the idea that she could be of help. If she had heard the weather forecasts with the tremendous torrential rains and seen video clips of the animals in their stalls, she might have run in the opposite direction. Perhaps this is why God wisely withholds so much from

us. Nonetheless, there she was on the ark. And, just as God would hope, she worked diligently to bring about the success of God's plan. Do we work just as diligently knowing that we are all part of God's plan for the earth? Is He waiting for us to show Him our tenacity before His blessings become known? While we do not know the answer to this, we do know that the traits of diligence and perseverance are highly revered in Scripture.

In Scripture we learn about these women and yet never know their names. Indeed, their names could be our names and our names could be theirs. These incredible women lent the physical and emotional support needed to attain victory for the Ark's purpose. As women, we know, or can certainly imagine, what had to be accomplished on that expedition. Laundry, toilets, and meals come quickly to mind. Add in the captivity, along with the animals, and we can all nod our heads in agreement, "Yes, we know what these women went through."

But so it was that from their tedium God saved humankind from extinction. From the monotony of their endless days caring for a multitude of animals and the daily needs of the people on the ark, these women ushered in the most beautiful of treasures. They help us realize that our daily tasks happen amidst many of God's miracles. They ushered in the continued existence of humanity. And yet we never learn their names. How might our existence mirror theirs? Let us look for the miracles that are happening all around us and thank God for them.

We can picture how these women would have worked tirelessly, side-by-side, with their spouses. Like us, they would have worked with a gratitude that could only come from understanding the innate value of what was being done but certainly there would have been times of emotional or physical exhaustion. That is why serving others is the ultimate gift of self—there can be no higher calling upon our lives. This is why Jesus made it clear that He came to serve, not be served; He who is King of Kings came to set an example of service. So when the men and women of the ark worked in union

with one another, the complementary nature of their relationship became apparent and how it was one of service became known.

We have to assume that the men and women, even in their exhaustion, would have found time for prayer and thanksgiving to the God who cared for them; the God we now serve and worship. This is the same loving God who set us upon our current path and associated us with our current friends and family. He is our tender God. He is our exacting Father. Like Noah's wife, even in our own exhaustion we are called upon to find time for prayer and thanksgiving—never really knowing how God is using us and our mundane actions but trusting that He is in such a way that we participate in building His kingdom.

Indeed, God's demands are very clear when we consider how arduous these women's lives must have been. We can understand His conditions when we consider that even with His concern for their survival, how much was required of them. It is the same with us. As we read in Ecclesiastes 3:2-8, we are reminded that our lives, too, will be filled with a variety of seasons. God gives each season, whether it is the time for weeping or the time for laughter, to us. And so, in looking to Noah's wife and daughters-in-law we can recognize these different seasons and know their necessity in God's plan. We can look to these women and understand that the seasons of our lives are a necessary part of our own survival, growth, and spiritual awakening.

Like these women, God cares for our physical survival and spiritual growth. However, for both of these to occur, we need to work persistently with Him, just as Noah's wife and daughters-in-law did. And in so doing we, too, must often find joy in the mundane. We, too, must look to a God who loves us immensely and find both our comfort and our peace in that knowledge. Whether it is our time to mourn or our time to dance, we must find solace in each season knowing that God is with us. He is a strong shoulder to cry on or a wonderful dance partner.

But how do we respond to God during the different seasons of our life? Do we remember that He has a bigger plan for us that we may not see? Do we work joyfully and persistently knowing that, in doing so, we glorify Him? Do we continue to love and worship Him through all the times of our life? Do we remember how important our work is even if we, too, forever remain nameless?

It is vital for us to remember that our contribution is no less valuable because of our anonymity. The world values notoriety and fame. God values our focus on Him and His call in our life. When we fully live and breathe for God, our life, and what we offer up with it, is as important as Noah's wife's life and the lives of his daughters-in-law. As wives, mothers, and cherished friends, our lives take on a new meaning when we look to these nameless, faceless, and yet ultimately amazing women for a renewed understanding of the treasure in our everyday tasks.

## *The Word of God*

*There is a time for everything, and a season for every activity under heaven:*

*A time to be born and a time to die,*
*A time to plant and a time to uproot,*
*A time to kill and a time to heal,*
*A time to tear down and a time to build,*
*A time to weep and a time to laugh,*
*A time to mourn and a time to dance,*
*A timer to scatter stones and a time to gather them,*
*A time to embrace and a time to refrain, a time to keep and a time to throw away,*
*A time to tear and a time to mend, a time to be silent and a time to speak,*
*A time to love and a time to hate,*
*A time for war and a time for peace.*

*Ecclesiastes 3:1-8*

*I know what it is to be in need, and I know what it is to have plenty. I have learned the secret of being content in any and every situation, whether well fed or hungry, whether living in plenty or in want. I can do everything through him who gives me strength. Philippians 4:12-13*

*I know that there is nothing better for men than to be happy and do good while they live. That everyone may eat and drink and find satisfaction in all his toil-this is the gift of God. Ecclesiastes 3:12-13*

*Do everything without grumbling or questioning, that you may be blameless and innocent, children of God without blemish in the midst of a crooked and perverse generation, among whom you shine like lights in the world, as you hold on to the world of life, so that my boast for the day of Christ may be that I did not run in vain or labor in vain. Philippians 2:14-16*

*Jesus' attitude to the women whom he meets in the course of his Messianic service reflects the eternal plan of God, who, in creating each one of them, chooses her and loves her in Christ.*

Mulieris Dignitatem

## *Sarah*

We are first introduced to Sarah in Genesis 11:29. Here we know her as Sarai, wife of Abram and daughter-in-law of Terah. Throughout the Genesis story we understand that Sarah is quite beautiful and seems to be a typical wife with longings to be a mother. It is important to understand that the physical attribute of beauty, in the Old Testament, is also a statement of righteousness, virtue, and often spiritual prowess. For Sarah these characteristics are evidenced by her role in the conversion of hundreds, maybe thousands, of people from pagan beliefs to monotheism as well as the fact that her tent was literally and figuratively open to all; welcoming and providing sustenance to any who were in need. She was a virtuous woman of God.

As the Genesis story progresses however, we learn that Sarah is barren. This becomes the focus of her existence as her longing for children continues to be unmet. Indeed, in the Scripture verse that lets us know of Sarah's barrenness, it also follows with an interesting four words: she had no children. This becomes a stark contrast to her other, godly characteristics and yet may also be fueled by her own husband's pursuit of the same thing: an heir to all he has been blessed with, through his own seed.

So, while in one way this double defined account (barren/had no children) looks like clarification on the statement regarding Sarah's

childlessness, in another way this looks like two different statements. In fact, the more we come to know Sarah, we can see that her treatment of Hagar, her maidservant, is seemingly without compassion—even if it appears justified due to Hagar's arrogance towards Sarah. In her blessings of a son and great wealth for her husband, she reacts with "barrenness" towards Hagar in wanting her expelled from the household. We see Sarah's complexity just as easily as we see our own. It is simple for us to sympathize with her and her situation. We are easily able to recall the times in our life when particular goals or interests have single-mindedly driven us forward or when we find it more than difficult—maybe even impossible—to react to certain situations with love and kindness.

Not only might Sarah remind us of ourselves and the barren times in our life, but she is also our mother in faith. It is from her lineage that we are able to trace ourselves back to Abraham and God's covenant. She will become the mother of the countless descendants that God promises Abraham. We will learn her story and witness how no one could replace her in this promise. And in that way, she is our foster mother, as we trace our faith back to the worship of the one true God, father of Jesus, triune with the Holy Spirit.

In Sarah we have a heroine who displays love, joy, doubt, jealousy and impatience. She is so very real and so very much like us. Recall that God promises Abram that Sarah will conceive, even though she is far past her childbearing years. Given her age, Sarah laughs at this promise from God. However, God is not offended by her reaction and we see His loving kindness as He fulfills His promise. The entire chain of events is meant to show us that nothing is ever too big, too far-fetched for God.

Sarah has a life filled with working with the Spirit of God and yet might possibly experience a "barrenness" and her faith waivers. Blessed Mother Teresa of Calcutta shared her own experiences with feelings of emptiness and personal quest in regards to her faith and relationship with God. At some point it only makes sense that Sarah

must have grappled with, and questioned, why she had never borne a child.

Yet we are duty bound to recall that she was considered, along with Abraham, to be a great converters of pagan people to the monotheistic religion of Judaism. Here is where her gift to Catholic women is quite immense. We live in a world where the secular is always pounding at our door; where keeping at bay the false idols of wealth, material gain, fame and the like is a daunting, if not overwhelming, task. Sarah's example to us is that we are called to be strong in the face of idol-worship—regardless of its presentation to our families and friends. Sarah, as a great converter of pagan people to monotheism, calls us to stand firm as we protect our families against the idol-worship that exists in the world in which we are raising our families.

Sarah also showed tremendous trust in God when she followed Abraham as he responded to God's call in Genesis 12:1 to "*Go forth from the land of your kinsfolk and from your father's house to a land I will show you.*" Indeed, throughout her life she put her faith in God in a way that we are all called to do but still had those times where her faith wasn't enough. Don't we all experience those droughts when our resolve seems to dissipate in the face of a particularly intimidating challenge or in our own selfish interests to blindly pursue a desire that we harbor in the depths of our hearts? So it may well have been for Sarah as she longed to have a child. Those longings took hold of her and could have easily shaken her faith in God. And yet she remained His faithful servant and He remained faithful to her! Sarah was so treasured in God's plan that Scripture recounts the blessings that Abraham gains because of Sarah.

In that way, Sarah helps us learn two very important aspects of God. First is the understanding that nothing is too tremendous, too austere for God. Second, that God never forgets His promises. But we see that Sarah both doubts and laughs at the prospect of God's promises, even after she has taken such an active role in bringing

the knowledge of a monotheistic God to a pagan nation. Like us, Sarah is multi-faceted. Don't we have times where we can feel our lives very much in sync with the Spirit and, paradoxically, experience times when we are filled with fear or jealousy or an emotion that really has no place if we fully trust in God?

How often do we, like Sarah, doubt that God will be true to us or true to His word? Or—maybe more appropriately—do we question **how** God can be faithful based upon our circumstances; just as Sarah questioned **how** she could conceive given her age and being long past child-bearing years.

How often have we lost our focus on what is set in Scripture and, instead, put it on what is set in the secular world? How often do we find ourselves being impatient in our circumstances instead of believing that we are right where God wants us to be? And finally, how often have we been forgiven by our merciful Father when we display the non-Christian characteristics of jealousy, resentment, and doubt?

As we read Sarah's story we know that she should hold out for the Lord's plan to unfold, but that is because we are privy to the ending. We know she will bear a son, just as God promised.

Sarah, however, being impatient and unable to wait for God's plan to unfold, insists that Abraham have relations with her maid Hagar. And, as a result of these relations, Hagar gives birth to Ishmael. Sarah's plan to bring children into Abraham's life seems to backfire, as Hagar appears to be boisterous at this new position in the household. Indeed, no one is pleased with the results of this plan. Abraham still cries out to God for an heir of his own seed and Sarah soon finds herself being taunted by Hagar in a way that undermines her own role as woman of the house, so to speak. Neither Sarah nor Abraham find resolve in the consequences of an action they took upon themselves to initiate.

It makes us ask ourselves: How often have we formulated the best of plans only to see them unfold in a less than desirable way? How often have we, like Sarah, moved ahead and not held out for the Lord's plan to evolve in His own time?

When our own self-interests are placed before God's will, we jeopardize our life's purpose; driven by our own desires only serves to separate us from God. This is why time spent in prayer, meditation, and studying Scripture allows us a deeper fellowship with our Creator. These things promulgate a rich, more personal relationship with God. From this point we are then able to live according to His edicts.

But like Sarah, we can most certainly think of countless times when our own excitement and anticipation cloud our decisions and we plow ahead with our own ideas, plans, and expectations. Probably more often than we know, our impatience has diminished the plans that the Lord has had in store for us. In learning about Sarah's journey (both physical and emotional) we are able to learn how we add both time and frustration to the events of our lives when we put our own interests before the Lord's interests.

Indeed, as Christian women, we can take so much from Sarah's story. We learn about God's commitment to us and His faithfulness to His covenant. In the end we witness His loving kindness in such a way that we ought to feel quite indebted. However all He really wants is our love, freely given.

There is simply no way for us to repay our Lord for all He does in our lives other than to use our free will in accepting and returning His unconditional love: the unconditional love so beautifully given to us in Jesus Christ. No debt is ever easier to repay than our debt to God through the acceptance of Jesus Christ.

Sarah's story shows us, in no uncertain terms, that our own focus can fog our vision of what really matters: trusting God. And yet, like Eve, Sarah's story tells of the Lord's commitment to His word even

when we do our best to jeopardize things. God so loves Sarah that He never forsakes her and we have that same place in His heart.

Consider the fact that even when Sarah scoffs at the idea that God will grant her a child in her old age, God is not put off. Indeed, the God we serve is always faithful to His declarations. And so Sarah gives birth to Isaac when she is ninety years old. The more we learn about God the more we will see that it makes perfect sense for Sarah to give birth at this very old age. In this, she cannot give credit to anyone other than God. At ninety years old, and with Abraham one hundred years old, we can be certain that Isaac's birth is a gift from God. We say this with an understanding that God's hand was fully part of this and not just as an esoteric remark. Make no mistakes about it, Sarah giving birth at ninety requires us to give all credit to God.

In the meantime, Abram and Hagar's son, Ishmael, was growing up. Remember that Ishmael had been born to Abram and Hagar when Sarah's impatience had gotten the better of her. Convinced that she would never have children, she encouraged Abram to have relations with her maid, Hagar. Now, for Sarah, the bitterness of this reminder of Abraham's other son, from a different woman, was too much for her to bear. Filled with frustration at Hagar's disrespect, and Ishmael's apparent interest in pagan women, Sarah orders Abraham to *"Get rid of that slave woman and her son, for the slave woman's son will never share in the inheritance with my son Isaac."* Genesis 21:10b

However, this chain of events with Sarah and Hagar must happen so that God's ultimate promise may come to be. God had made a covenant with Abraham and told him that he would be the father of many nations. That would happen with Sarah and not Hagar.

Nonetheless, we shudder at the realization that Sarah's original interference in God's plan brought about this climactic result to Hagar and her son. Had Sarah had the patience and faith that what

God promised would come to pass, then she would not have asked

Abraham to have relations with Hagar. And, of course, the ensuing frustration would have not taken place.

In our life we undoubtedly cause trouble or sadness to others. Whether intentional or not, through our own greed, impatience, or thoughtlessness we have certainly been the cause of pain or anguish. We are probably aware of most of these occasions as they happen or very shortly thereafter. Hopefully, as we grow in our faith, we are developing a compassion towards others that diminishes our capacity to inflict such unkindness. We become aware of how our actions affect other people.

On the other hand, Sarah's story gives us insight into the times where our actions cause pain and we remain unaware—even if they seem warranted or justified. She makes us take note of those remorseful times, which may very well be revealed to us at the end of our life, when the knowledge of how we have hurt or saddened others is beyond remedy. Our awareness of the error of Sarah's mistreatment of Hagar—even if we consider it justified because of Hagar's disrespect—should be reflected in our daily life as we act more conscientiously in words and deeds; but, it should also reflect the fact that God's own commitment to us, Jesus Christ, beseeches us to us our free will in such a way as to have an attitude of love and compassion to all.

We must ask ourselves, how many times have we been in that same situation? Our lives are working well: we have our health, our family, and our friends. We have food to eat and share laughter with others. And still, gratitude doesn't fill our hearts. So it is that Sarah again shows us that even when God keeps His word and blesses our lives, we are sometimes less than grateful. We, too, find ourselves forgetting to look at what we have and mistakenly choose to focus on what we don't have.

In fact, Sarah's life was changed so much that God changed her name as well. Sarai became Sarah. Abram became Abraham. We, too, have most certainly experienced those life-changing moments.

They might come in the form of the birth of a child, a near fatal accident, or the acquisition of a new and rewarding opportunity. We want to move forward, feel ready to forge ahead, and yet find some of our old "selves" still surfacing. So it was with Sarah. Regardless of her good fortune she still experiences a sort of jealousy towards Hagar. She still exhibits such unkindness towards Hagar that an angel of the Lord must reassure Hagar that she is being heard.

Sarah allows us to meditate on the barrenness in our lives and know that, even in the driest of times, God is with us. She forces us to ask ourselves difficult questions: How often are our emotions barren? In what circumstances is jealousy or impatience driving our decisions? And in these situations, how can we return to God and His caring arms? Although we are on our own sovereign journeys, our paths are continuously crossed with others' paths. How we interact and influence others will speak of our love for Jesus. Being part of a community provides opportunity for us to develop a loving and compassionate attitude towards all people.

In Scripture we are told that how we treat others is how we are treating Jesus. Jesus asks us how we would be able to love a God that we cannot see when we can't even love the people that we can see. Sarah reminds us of this dilemma.

Clearly we serve a God whose love is so absolute that even in our ungratefulness it cannot be diminished. Sarah assists us in attaining the full realization that God's love is unconditional regardless of our "humanness." Sarah's life resounds with beauty for us because she is so very real, so very temporal, and so very blessed by God. There is great comfort in the knowledge that even in our most transient of moments, our God never abandons us.

Sarah, then, prods us to stay the course with God. She teaches us the value of patience and the need for loving-kindness to others. Her story resounds with the knowledge that, even if we try to alter or direct circumstances, no one can take our place in God's plan.

Hagar simply could not replace Sarah in God's plan and promise to Abraham. But God would not abandon Hagar either. She also became part of the plan.

In the end, we see that her life changes in ways so great that God changes her name as well. Sarai becomes Sarah. She is reborn in Him just as we are reborn in Christ. A beautiful moment indeed: both for Sarah and for ourselves. Through Sarah we are reminded of God's great love for us and how He will always be true to His commitment. In this knowledge, we are given all the more reason to study and learn His edicts, His ways.

When we understand how to work with Him and the Holy Spirit, our lives become filled with purpose. We live, then, as we ought to live: for Him and His glory. We do well when we remind ourselves that the word of God remains as true today, as beautiful today, as it was thousands of years ago. He remains as true to us as He was to Sarah. We see that staying faithful to God, in being strong against the idols of our world—fame, fortune, attainment of material goods, improper or wasteful use of our time—we become like Sarah and help our friends and families stay faithful to the one true Savior, Jesus Christ.

*On her account it went very well with Abram, and he received flocks and herds, male and female slaves, male and female asses, and camels. Genesis 12:16*

*God also said to Abraham, "As for Sarai your wife, you are no longer to call her Sarai; her name will be Sarah. I will bless her and will surely give you a son by her. I will bless her so that she will be the mother of nations; kings of people will come from her. Genesis 17:15-16*

*Remember this: Whoever sows sparingly will also reap sparingly, and whoever sows generously will also reap generously. 2 Corinthians 9:6*

*In your anger do not sin. Do not let the sun go down while you are still angry, and do not give the devil a foothold. Ephesians 4:26-27*

*The matter distressed Abraham greatly because it concerned his son. But God said to him, "Do not be so distressed about the boy and your maid-servant. Listen to whatever Sarah tells you, because it is through Isaac that your offspring will be reckoned. I will make the son of the maidservant into a nation also, because he is your offspring. Genesis 21:11-13*

*Let those who love the Lord hate evil, for he guards the lives of his faithful ones and delivers them from the hand of the wicked. Psalm 97:10*

*Now the Lord was gracious to Sarah, as he had said, and the Lord did for Sarah what he had promised. Sarah became pregnant and bore a son to Abraham in his old age, at the very time God had promised him. Genesis 21: 1-2*

*All of God's action in human history at all times respects the free will of the human "I."*

Mulieris Dignitatem

## Lot's Wife

The genealogy in Scripture is both fascinating and a bit confusing for those of us not considered Biblical Scholars. For instance, most of us know the story of Lot but do not know that Lot was Abraham's nephew. Lot's father, Haran, was Abraham's brother. Or we may recall that Lot's wife was turned to a pillar of salt but not know that Lot was quite wealthy when he and Abraham went their separate ways: with Lot settling near the city of Sodom.

What we know about Lot's wife is little indeed and yet what we can learn from her is immense. Here is a woman whose family lives in a city where debauchery, greed, and licentiousness are prevalent. Essentially, Sodom could represent any fair city today that is operating outside of God's laws. It might be my city; it might be your city. So, like Lot's wife, many of us probably live within cities that are an affront to the Lord.

And, like Lot's wife, we have come to know and cherish our lives within these cities. We may watch the news and be appalled by the happenings within our city limits but, for the most part, tend to continue living in our cities. We would be hard pressed to move or to imagine ourselves elsewhere. Where we live is a part of who we are and creates the fabric of our existence. We seek out the good and try to remedy or disregard the bad.

It would seem fair to assume that Lot's wife had the same kind of feelings towards her city and home that we have about our cities

and our homes. Maybe she chose to see the worthy and tried to disregard the wicked. Even when she was led from her city by an angel of God and told not to look back, her sadness, regret, or even curiosity got the better of her.

Imagine what her reaction would have been when she learned she had to leave her city, her home. It would have been only human to feel opposition to such an idea. We have all read countless stories of people who refused to be evacuated, who choose to take their chances against impending doom: whether it be from hurricanes, floods, tornadoes, or volcanoes. Maybe Lot's wife was like that. Like most people in the same situation, she probably left grudgingly, unwillingly. And, in her grief, or because of her curiosity and emotions, she made the fatal mistake to look back at what was being left behind—even when she knew better.

Our lives are packed with the same predicament: God tries to move us forward but we keep looking back. We are often driven by our emotions as they are attached to different times and experiences. Although the idea of looking back so that we are able to move forward in a positive way is certainly commendable, for the most part we tend to look back unproductively. And, like Lot's wife, our lives are often in ruins because of this instinct, this longing, and this habit to look over our shoulder at what "was." Like Peter, who loses his footing when he takes his eyes off Jesus, we, too, lose our way when we take our eyes off God. Our eyes should stay fixed on God who is doing His very best to save us, often from ourselves.

We should not be surprised that God will always do what He has to do in order to deliver us from impending disaster. What should surprise us is how often He will try, given our stubbornness to attempt to do things our way and to settle things according to our will. Haven't we all faced circumstances that we would prefer to avoid, believing our knowledge was the ultimate knowledge and our plan the better plan? Isn't there a time when life has made us move in one direction when we would have preferred another? But when we are living for God we can trust His word that all things will work

for His good. With that knowledge, that trust, comes our ability to be led by His Spirit into new and uncharted territories.

When we trust God we are able to move in those intimidating times. In His love our fears do not immobilize us. With our confidence placed firmly in Him we are able to let go of the past, knowing that all it held has brought us to this place with Him, right here, right now. We must always believe in His providence and have faith in His ultimate love for us. And so, when guided by the Spirit, we progress, we forge ahead. And, like Lot's wife, we are better to leave the past behind. We need to keep our eye on the future and our focus on God.

But do we look back? Of course we do. And don't these glimpses of the past haunt us? They most certainly do. But Lot's wife is here to remind us, in no uncertain terms, that the past is just that: past. The purpose of our past is that we learn from it but that we also be willing to give it over to God when it is too much to bear. In that way we are able to be most fully alive in the present, which is truly a gift from God.

Did Lot's wife suffer the ultimate consequences for that brief glimpse of what she was leaving behind? She did. And don't we, when we nurture that part of ourselves that finds comfort in our own sorrows, or our own martyrdoms, also suffer consequences? We absolutely do. Are they the ultimate consequences? They are in that they keep us from living for God's glory in the here and now. They hinder us from the joy that God has in mind for our lives. And in that way, they continually alter our relationship with God.

Consider the time we spend nursing old wounds as if our very life depended on them. Too often we use them as excuses for our current dilemmas. We don't want to learn from them but prefer to lean on them. We nurture them, tend to them, and stash them away for a rainy day. We don't allow them to die for fear we will need them. We allow them to fester until they become ailments in our physical bodies. We allow those wounds, instead of the Holy Spirit,

to take hold of us and lead our tomorrows. Too much of the time that should be given to God, and to the people He has brought into our lives, is spent in idle pity or in sorrow for what might have been or what will never be.

Does this mean we shouldn't allow ourselves to rightfully mourn certain things in our lives? Of course it doesn't. There are volumes of works published on the healing characteristics of forgiveness. Let us remind ourselves that Jesus came for those of us who need His healing, whether physical or emotional. It would be foolish for us to abandon this offering.

Indeed, we should turn over our repentant or saddened hearts to Him. We should learn from our past experiences, whether perpetuated by us or upon us, and create a better future for ourselves through Christ. We should also loosen our grip on our old wounds. Let us enjoin our tragedies and sadness with the death of Jesus on the cross. And in so doing, we place these things at Christ's feet where they might be washed away in the blood and water of His wounds.

This allows us, then, a starting point, our own earthly resurrection, in which we will be able to enjoy God's gift of life and friendship in new and deeper ways. And as those wounds resurface, because they most assuredly will, we continually give them over to Jesus. In that way we show, through our words and our spiritual actions, our complete trust in Him.

As often happens, the Old Testament foreshadows messages in the New Testament. We might consider the message of Lot's wife, with its dire consequences, to be a forerunner to the simple but succinct verse regarding Simon's mother-in-law. That same message of "letting go and moving on" is made rather quickly in Luke 4:38-39.

*Jesus left the synagogue and went to the home of Simon. Now Simon's mother-in-law was suffering from a high fever, and they*

*asked Jesus to help her. So he bent over her and rebuked the fever, and it left her. She got up at once and began to wait on them.*

We don't read that they all sat around and marveled at what had just happened. Simon's mother-in-law didn't go on and on about her near death experience. In fact, it is quite telling that there were no reactions whatsoever. Indeed, the faith of those who asked Jesus for His help was such that they simply knew it would be forthcoming and successful. Business was at hand. It, once again, shows us the reciprocal nature of our relationship with Christ. On the one hand He **does** for us so that we can **do** for others. On the other hand when we **do** for others we open the floodgates for Him to **do** for us. It becomes all about "doing," about action.

When Lot's wife looks back, she reflects the time in a woman's life when the emotional component of her actions speaks louder than reason—and sometimes reason needs to prevail. The upside of women being much attuned with their feminine, emotional side is the way in which they can "read" a situation and respond. The downside of this emotional aspect of a woman's gifts is when that emotional nature isn't held in-check—when it rules what she does without wisdom or understanding. In this way, the Creator's plan is that men and women work together to bring out the best in one another. A man often offers a woman a sense of emotional balance while a woman offers a man a sense of the mystical aspects of heaven and earth—a chance to experience the world more intuitively and thus more vibrantly.

When a woman is completely run by her emotions, when there is no male complement to what she says and does, the consequences can be deadly; this can be literally or figuratively. Writes von Hildebrand:

*How beautiful is the complementariness of men and women according to the Divine Plan. It is not by accident that Saint Francis of Assisi was best understood by Saint Clare; Saint Francis of Sales by Saint Jeanne Francoise de Chantal; Saint Vincent of Paul by Louise de*

*Marillac. In our own times, Marie Pila was co-foundress with Father Eugene Marie of Notre Dame de Vie in the Provence. Man is made for communion and the most perfect form of communion calls for persons who complement each other.*

Shamefully, this recognition of how male and female are able to balance and complement one another has been seen as a "weakness" on the part of a woman when, in fact, it takes a strong person to recognize her own weaknesses! Just as St. Paul tells us in 2 Corinthians 12:10:

*Therefore, I am content with weaknesses, insults, hardships, persecution and constraints, for the sake of Christ; for when I am weak, I am strong.*

While we certainly value the ability to "pick ourselves up by the bootstraps," if that attitude becomes an air of complete self-reliance in which God's role is diminished or shut out, it quickly becomes a way in which we separate ourselves from our Creator. Rather, it is better to see in our weaknesses how we depend upon God.

When the faith in our heart is strong, love is balanced through complementary relationships with compassion and wisdom to drive our actions. It is as if we can't do enough for others because our love for Jesus, and seeing Him in everyone, propels us forward. We have gratitude for those people in our lives that bring us balance and are better able to move forward so that we can pray for others, counsel others, help one another, and show compassion and mercy. We live for Christ in the purest of ways. We don't lose today's opportunities to yesterday's pain, sorrow, or regret. We become thankful for what the past held—and what we learned from it—and then express gratitude for a new day to glorify the Lord. Our emotions can serve us and serve God but do not rule us.

Simon's mother-in-law shows us, like Lot's wife, that our goal is to move forward to do the work of Jesus, whatever that might entail. For her, it was caring for those around her. For us it might be the

same but in a different capacity; maybe as a supervisor or as a colleague. However, we live in a secular world that gives us a message that is in direct opposition to the message in Scripture. We are often encouraged to win-at-all-costs or to accept callousness as a "life lesson." Through Scripture passages, however, we are encouraged to take the spotlight off of ourselves and shine it on others who might benefit from our care, our time, and our focus. We can surely count on God's Word that in that way we are ultimately helping ourselves. He knows what works!

Lot's wife, just like Simon's mother-in-law, prods us to let our yesterdays go. She reminds us that, in looking back, we sacrifice the future. A future meant for God. Without ambiguity, Lot's wife forces our focus ahead, leaving what should be behind us, behind us. Combined with Jesus' death on the cross, we should allow the pain or sadness from our yesterdays to be washed away in His blood. We then can eagerly anticipate each day as a chance to live in the joy and peace that Jesus gave us through His death and resurrection.

## *The Word of God*

*He approached, grasped her hand, and helped her up. Then the fever left her and she waited on them. Mark 1:31*

*But Jesus told him, "Follow me, and let the dead bury their own dead." Matthew 8:22*

*No one who puts his hand to the plow and looks back is fit for service in the kingdom of God. Luke 9:62*

*The seed is the word of God. Those along the path are the ones who hear, and then the devil comes and takes away the word from their hearts, so that they may not believe and be saved. Those on the rock are the ones who receive the word with joy when they hear it, but they have no root. They believe for a while, but in the time of testing they fall away. The seed that fell among thorns stands for those who hear, but as they go on their way they are choked by life's worries, riches, and pleasures, and they do not mature. But the seed on good soil stands for those with a noble and good heart, who hear the word, retain it, and by persevering produce a good crop. Luke 8:11-15*

*Cast all your anxiety on him because he cares for you. 1 Peter 5:7*

*Then the Lord rained down burning sulfur on Sodom and Gomorrah-from the Lord out of the heavens. Thus he overthrew those cities and the entire plain, including all those living in the cities-and also the vegetation in the land. But Lot's wife looked back, and she became a pillar of salt. Genesis 19:24-26*

*Forget the former things; do not dwell on the past. See, I am doing a new thing! Now it springs up; do you not perceive it? Isaiah 43:18-19*

*Thus in the same context as the creation of man and woman, the biblical account speaks of God's instituting marriage as an indispensable condition for the transmission of life to new generations, the transmission of life to which marriage and conjugal love are by their nature ordered: "Be fruitful and multiply, and fill the earth and subdue it."*

Mulieris Dignitatem

## *Rebekah*

Rebekah is Sarah's daughter-in-law. She married Sarah's beloved son, Isaac. When we read Genesis we can't help but notice that there are many similarities between Sarah and Rebekah—both are strong women, protective of their households and attuned to God and His will. Additionally, we know that as the wife of Isaac, it is with Rebekah that the Lord will continue delivering His promise. The covenant He made with Abraham that his descendents would be more numerous than the stars in the sky will proceed with Rebekah as Isaac's wife.

Rebekah's story actually begins with Abraham's search for a wife for his son, Isaac. In his old age Abraham sent his chief servant on this mission. Abraham made his servant promise to go back to the land of Abraham's relatives. Abraham did not want his servant to find a wife from among the Canaanite women. Abraham's allegiance was with the God of his ancestors: our God, the one true God. And so his servant went, with as much trust in Abraham as Abraham had in God.

For her part we have to assume that Rebekah was also a trusting and allegiant young woman. We are able to marvel at how God's plan unfolded for her. She shows us how God is always in the smallest

details of our lives. Here we have a number of young women going to a well to draw water right at the moment that Abraham's servant is at the well. We hear the servant asking the God of Abraham to make it clear if any of the women at the well is called to be the one for whom he was sent—the one who would become Isaac's wife.

Rebekah is that woman. She has many traits that make her the fulfillment of God's plan for His people. Rebekah is filled with compassion, strength, and loving-kindness; often called *chesed.* Rebekah is from the family necessary to be a suitable wife for Isaac but also must willingly accept the marriage offer. Her father is Nahor, Abraham's brother. The entire scene at the well, which prepares us to join Rebekah's journey towards Isaac and to take her place in the line of Jewish Matriarchs, is one filled with anticipation and excitement.

Rebekah's traits of compassion, strength, and chesed are witnessed by her offer of water to both Abraham's servant but also in offering water for his camels. This is no easy task to be accomplished and takes the combination of all three traits to be successful. Her compassion and chesed would have been the impetus for her to make these offers to the stranger and her strength would have allowed her to work the well in such a way as to supply water to camels—known to hold tremendous amounts of the liquid—thus requiring an arduous commitment on Rebekah's part to fill.

Recall, also, that Abraham sent his servant in complete faith that God would guide the journey. Abraham's servant had that same complete faith in Abraham, and subsequently Abraham's God. Rebekah must also have had the same faith as she listened to the servant's story of his assignment and accepted the proposal. This total faith in God is shown to us, over and over again, throughout Scripture. Faith, we read, heals. Faith, we learn, moves mountains. Faith, we witness, brings salvation.

Throughout the story we see that there are numerous ways in which Isaac and Rebekah's life mirrors Abraham and Sarah's. As well as being barren like Sarah, the beautiful Rebekah was the cause of a lie that Isaac felt he had to make regarding Rebekah's identity when they were in the foreign land of Gerar. In Gerar, Isaac tells the men that Rebekah is his sister. He does this because he believes that the men might kill him to have Rebekah, should they know that Rebekah is his wife. Not until the king of the Philistines, Abimelech, sees Isaac caressing Rebekah is their lie uncovered. At this point the king orders that both Isaac and Rebekah should remain untouched and unharmed. To make himself clear, the king announces that anyone disobeying this order would be put to death. This is quite similar to Abraham's lie regarding Sarah's identity when they were in Egypt (Genesis 12:10-20). Ultimately, like Sarah before her, Rebekah's presence in a foreign land becomes the reason for safe passage and the eventual fulfillment of God's plan.

It is an interesting statement that the beauty of each woman was, at first, cause for concern on her husband's part, and then became the reason for their safe existence in an alien environment.

It was a woman whose existence ushered in protection for God's plan to continue to manifest. It was imperative that Rebekah's offspring, in lineage with Sarah, inherit the promise of great blessings from God. Once again, we are reminded that each one of us has a unique calling that no one else can fill. Each of us, whether we remain anonymous or draw fame, is an active part of God's plan. If we do not fulfill our purpose, no one else will. And so, these women who are our ancestors in faith, remind us to stay true to God knowing and believing that He is working in our lives.

Not only was Rebekah, like Sarah, considered to be quite beautiful but she was also barren. So, as did his father before him, Isaac *prayed to the Lord on behalf of his wife, because she was barren* (Genesis 25:21).

Rebekah's circumstances, like Sarah's, give us a powerful example of intercessory prayer. While our personal relationship with Jesus allows us to turn to Him with our joy, our sadness, and our hopes

there are also times when we should heed the value of intercession. There are times that our supplications, along with others' on our behalf, become powerful indeed. And, of course, the reverse is true. We should understand the need and triumphant nature of our intercession for others. So, when Isaac prays to the Lord to open Rebekah's womb, we see firsthand the intrinsic value of intercessory prayer. Along with feeding the hungry and clothing the naked we should always understand the value of praying for others. In that way we are raising each other to the Lord, for His care and His mercy.

As a result of Isaac's prayer, Rebekah becomes pregnant with twins. As events unfold we find that these twins, Jacob and Esau, develop very different personalities: Esau, the first born, becomes a skillful hunter while Jacob, the second born, grows into a quiet, somewhat reflective man. As young men we learn that these very diverse personalities each draw a different parent into favoritism. Rebekah favors Jacob while Isaac favors Esau.

When we next encounter Rebekah, her children are grown. She is eavesdropping on a conversation that Esau is having with Isaac. Isaac is instructing Esau to go and hunt some wild game and prepare it for Isaac. Isaac wants to enjoy the meal and give Esau his blessing. Isaac knows that he is nearing the end of his life and wants to put his estate in order, so to speak. This includes giving Esau the blessing customarily meant for the first born. Isaac wants to make sure he does this before he dies.

Because Rebekah seemingly favors Isaac, she intentionally undermines the blessing that Isaac intended for Esau. In doing this she ensures that Jacob inherits the sanctification meant for Esau. Rebekah devises a ruse in which Jacob misleads his father into believing that he is Esau (as Isaac is too old to see) and subsequently "steals" Esau's blessing.

Jewish teachings on Rebekah add a necessary depth to the understanding of this Matriarch. According to many such writings,

Rebekah understood that Jacob was more spiritually attuned than Esau and would, therefore, be able to most completely fulfill the role that God had ordained for the lineage of Abraham. She saw that her hand was needed in directing the outcome of the situation. God must have counted on her and in that way His will was done. This is supported by Scripture (Genesis 25:22-23) that clearly indicates how Rebekah becomes privy to God's plan and thus requires actions from her that will guarantee its success.

Rebekah, then, very clearly shows us the two sides of ourselves. Both that side that is able to work with the Holy Spirit and accept the path that we are on as well as the side that is able to take matters into our own hands. Rebekah's story encourages us to prayerfully move through our lives, learning the word of God and developing a deep, passionate relationship with Jesus. And in so doing, know that we are to be ever watchful of our steps and yet trusting that they are in sync with our Creator when we ask Him to lead the way.

Rebekah gives us a beautiful example of that trust when she accepts Abraham's servant's offer at the well. She then shows us her "lioness" instincts as a mother when she intervenes on Jacob's behalf. Certainly, after contemplating the entire story of Esau and Jacob, we can assume that God chose Rebekah because He could count on her ability to determine the times to react and the times to accept. Rebekah is our beautiful example of working with God—something we cannot mirror if we choose to ignore or deny our female gifts and mistakenly believe that we are less valuable than men because we are different! Rebekah shows that the difference is both necessary and natural and that when we are in sync with ourselves, as women, there is very little that we can't accomplish.

In the New Testament, Rebekah's skill at reading and knowing how to work with God is reiterated in the story of Mary and Martha (Luke 10:38-41). Both women are in the company of Jesus. Mary sits at His feet, understanding her call at that moment. Martha, on the other hand, busies herself. She is most certainly preparing food and drink. As Martha complains to Jesus that Mary is not being

helpful, Jesus quickly says that it is Mary who is reacting correctly in the given circumstances. So here we have two women in the exact same moment in time but with different responses. The story very clearly shows us that our walk with God requires our understanding of each step along the way. When we continue to develop our relationship with Him, through prayer, anointed friendships, and learning His word, we are more apt to make the right choices, like Mary, in our day-to-day lives.

We look to these women: Rebekah, Mary, and Martha to gain insight into knowing God and following His Spirit. We see the value of loving-kindness and compassion as we choose to live like Rebekah and be able to respond to any opportunity God presents to fulfill His plan. It is that same chesed that allows us to follow the Spirit like Mary did as she sat at Christ's feet. And when we revert to our Martha ways, we are able to find great peace in Christ as He patiently takes our hand and leads us on. And we smile, knowingly, at how Martha responded because we can be so much like her! Indeed, it is often easier to be Martha than to be Mary, and yet when we live in the Spirit, making those distinctions becomes less complicated in our everyday lives.

All these women provide us with inspiration to live in accordance to the priorities of God. We also learn the need for intercessory prayer, both on our behalf and ours on the behalf of others. Most importantly, we learn the value of working with God and taking our lead from Him, according to His word. This is evidenced quite clearly in Rebekah's story, specifically in Genesis 24:21 when we are made fully aware of the need to spend time in silence to "hear" God's response to our prayers, being able to accept that the silence may be a minute, an hour, a month or seemingly a lifetime.

These women help us learn to act and react in ways that are pleasing to God and fulfilling to ourselves.

*The man watched her the whole time, silently waiting to learn whether or not the Lord had made his errand successful. Genesis 24:21*

*The babies jostled each other within her, and she said, "Why is this happening to me?" So she went to inquire of the Lord. The Lord said to her, "Two nations are in your womb, and two peoples from within you will be separated; one people will be stronger than the other, and the older will serve the younger." Genesis 25:22-23*

*For sin is not to have any power over you, since you are not under the law but under grace. Romans 6:14*

*Then he prayed, "O Lord, God of my master Abraham, give me success today, and show kindness to my master Abraham. See, I am standing beside this spring, and the daughters of the townspeople are coming out to draw water. May it be that when I say to a girl, 'Please let down your jar that I may have a drink,' and she says, 'Drink, and I'll water your camels too'-let her be the one you have chosen for your servant Isaac. By this I will know that you have shown kindness to my master." Genesis 24:12-14*

*Then Isaac took Rebekah into his tent; he married her, and thus she became his wife. In his love for her Isaac found solace after the death of his mother Sarah. Genesis 24:67*

*Therefore will I proclaim you, O Lord, among the nations, and I will sing praise to your name. 2 Samuel 22:50*

*Then he turned toward the woman and said to Simon, "Do you see this woman? I came into your house. You did not give me any water for my feet, but she wet my feet with her tears and wiped them with her hair. You did not give me a kiss, but this woman, from the time I entered, has not stopped kissing my feet. You did not put oil on my head, but she has poured perfume on my feet. Therefore, I tell you, her many sins have been forgiven-for she loved much..." Luke 7:44-47*

*It is evident that women are meant to form part of the living and working structure of Christianity in so prominent a manner that perhaps not all their potentialities have yet been made clear.*

Mulieris Dignitatem

## *Rachel*

Rachel became Rebekah's daughter-in-law when she married Rebekah's favored son, Jacob. Rachel appears to be, by all accounts, a strong-willed, solid-minded young lady. Her nerve and her conviction are quite admirable and set the tone for her self-confident approach to God.

Like Sarah and Rebekah before her, Rachel is unable to conceive. However, whereas Abraham and Isaac call upon the Lord to open their wives' wombs, Rachel herself implores the Lord for a child. Here we see the wife of Jacob, heir to the Lord's promises, taking matters into her own hands. She needs no intercessor. She is able bodied and confident enough to know what she wants and go about getting it. Rachel is a woman with many admirable traits. Traits that we know are valued in Scripture. She is strong, resilient, and sure of herself in God. She shows us that even as early as Genesis, the Lord is giving us beautiful examples of women who are capable and bold.

Rachel easily assumes her own right to call upon God to fulfill her most heartfelt desire: to have a child. As such, Rachel's story empowers all women in their right to stand before God and seek their heart's desires. This has been given to us through Christ's blood.

However, there are often times when we feel burdened by our guilt or unworthy to make request of God. We should always remember that through the redemption of Jesus and with a repentant heart, our God welcomes a dialogue with us. So, while we see through Sarah and Rebekah that there are times when intercession is necessary and desirable, we witness through Rachel the times when intercession is unnecessary and we are emboldened to stand before God with our gratitude, our hopes, and our prayers.

When living lives guided by the Holy Spirit we are more capable of discerning these moments where we can confidently approach God. We learn through contemplative actions to listen to the still, small voice that tugs at our heart and guides us. We learn to know when our hopes and dreams are in keeping with God's will in our life. And from that knowledge we acquire the confidence that comes from walking with God who desires complete fellowship with each of us.

It is no wonder that we are drawn to Rachel's strength just as Jacob must have been. Nor is it out of character that Jacob's relationship with Rachel also began without intercession. Whereas Abraham sent his servant to find a wife for Isaac, Isaac simply sent Jacob on his way to find a wife. Isaac's only parting remarks to Jacob were, just as Abraham's wishes were for Isaac:

*Do not marry a Canaanite woman. Go at once to Paddan Aram, to the house of your mother's father Bethuel. Take a wife for yourself there, from among the daughters of Laban, your mother's brother. May God Almighty bless you and make you fruitful and increase your numbers until you become a community of peoples. Genesis 28:1-3*

While Jacob was his mother's favorite because of his mild manner (remember that he was a man of the tents—a "homebody" with a great intuitive, sensitive side—his brother Esau was a hunter) it is easy to see why he would have been so drawn to Rachel. Indeed their meeting was, just like Rebekah and Isaac's, one of love at first sight; at least on the side of Jacob! Meeting her at a well, just as his

mother was at a well and accepted the marriage offer made on Isaac's behalf; Rachel, too, exhibited the same qualities of strength, chesed, and compassion. Indeed, she was self-assured and competent as she alone tended the flock in her role as young shepherdess.

As we have often heard, opposites tend to attract and with that, we have an interesting, vibrant Old Testament marriage. We know from Scripture that Jacob so loved Rachel that, after having worked seven years as his 'bride price' for her, and then being tricked into marrying her older sister Leah, he quickly committed to another seven years so that he might still marry Rachel. Her countenance was such that Jacob could not walk away from her. Instead, he willingly gave another chunk of his life to her father who was, by all accounts, a deceitful man.

Eventually Rachel and Jacob marry and Rachel's longing for a child fuels a competition with her sister, Leah. It seems especially consoling to see that when the women in the Bible display the same characteristics and emotions that we exhibit, like envy or jealousy, our magnificent God still loves them unconditionally. And from that we know that He loves us too, in all our weaknesses and faults.

Hopefully we can also see from this particular heart-wrenching saga of jealous competition that, with God, there is enough anointing, enough blessings for everyone. It would seem that a state of envy is, in fact, a statement of disbelief or distrust in God's plan for us. Envy essentially translates into a declaration to God that sounds like, *"I'm not happy or content with where I am in life or what I have."* This is really not an assertion we want to make. Preferably we want to move forward in gratitude and faith, believing that God is working in our lives and His omniscience is to be trusted.

When Rachel finally gives birth it is to the beloved Joseph, the favored son of Jacob. It is Rachel to whom the Gospel of Matthew refers in 2:18. Here Matthew is telling about the birth of Jesus, the

way in which the Magi deceived Herod, and the ensuing consequences: all Hebrew boys under two years old were to be killed. Matthew tells us that what the prophet Jeremiah said had been fulfilled.

*A voice was heard in Ramah, sobbing and loud lamentation; Rachel weeping for her children, and she would not be consoled, since they were no more.*

In this way Rachel is intimately connected to Mary, mother of Jesus, as well. Just as Rachel's soul would mourn the terrible massacre of infant boys in Bethlehem, Mary would mourn the devastating crucifixion of her son. Indeed, her heart would be pierced.

So in Rachel we are presented with a wonderfully strong, capable woman who quite confidently stands before God with her hopes and dreams. But we also see a woman whose soul would experience great pain in the slaughter, generations later, of Hebrew babies. She is, as most of us are, a complex woman: strong enough to stand before the Lord and make her requests known but fragile in her heart as she weeps for the massacred babies. She exhibits the tremendous strength that so many of us possess and teaches us to pursue our heart's desire when it is surely in keeping with God. Ultimately reminding us that it is, as we have been told, in our heart that the Father seeks us.

Just as we saw Rachel confidently going to the Lord in the Old Testament, we have the bleeding woman approaching the Lord in the New Testament. She boldly pushes through a crowd to touch the edge of Jesus' cloak. Like Rachel before her, this woman intrinsically knows the importance of her own responsibility in her life. She goes after what she wants and believes that she will receive it. This particular woman knows that if she only touches Jesus' robe, she will experience the healing she has sought for a dozen years. She goes right to the source.

This is a perfect understanding of Jesus in our life. He is completely "there" for us. We might get jostled along the way, but when we persevere, we find success. Making the effort to move ourselves forward only speaks of our unwavering faith: a sure pleasure to Jesus.

As a word of caution, in the story of the persistent widow we hear the Lord say, "*...However, when the Son of Man comes, will he find faith on the earth?*" Luke 18:8. He is asking us, challenging us, to put our faith under a microscope. He wants us to examine our faith in light of our life's circumstances. Do we maintain our faith when the chips are down? Do we rally around our Creator when it seems as if He is nowhere to be found? These are the times that we show our true faith. This is why Scripture values traits like perseverance and diligence. When we endure through our difficulties, having faith in the Father, then we are professing our unwavering belief in Him.

We should then, like Rachel and the bleeding woman, show faith through our bold confidence in approaching the Lord and trusting in His presence. It is through our experiences, and uncertain or distressing times, which we are able to further develop and enjoy a mutually loving relationship with God. We are not, then, faith-weather friends. We know and savor the bond that exists between Creator and creation because we have participated in its development. Nothing separates us, or keeps us, from God's love and His working in our life. We then confidently stand before the Lord: faithfully loving and trusting Him.

## *The Word of God*

*And in his name the Gentiles will hope. Matthew 12:21*

*Lord my God, in you I take refuge. Psalm 7:2*

*She said to herself, "If only I can touch his cloak, I shall be cured." Matthew 9:21*

*If you wish to return, O Israel, say the Lord, return to me. Jeremiah 4:1*

*Invoking a blessing on Rebekah, they said: "Sister, may you grow into thousands of myriads; And may your descendants gain possession of the gates of their enemies!" Genesis 24:60*

*Then God remembered Rachel; he listened to her and opened her womb. She became pregnant and gave birth to a son and said, "God has taken away my disgrace." She named him Joseph, and said, "May the Lord add to me another son." Genesis 30:22-24*

*As Jesus was on his way, the crowds almost crushed him. And a woman who was bleeding for twelve years, but no one could heal her. She came up behind him and touched the edge of his cloak and immediately her bleeding stopped. Luke 8:42-44*

*The Lord does not look at the things man looks at. Man looks at the outward appearance, but the Lord looks at the heart. 1 Samuel 16:7b*

*You are my lamp, O Lord! Oh my God, you brighten the darkness about me. 2 Samuel 22:29*

*From the beginning of Christ's mission, women show to him and to his mystery a special sensitivity which is characteristic of their femininity.*

Mulieris Dignitatem

## *Leah*

The Jewish home is filled with wonder and awe as the Sabbath is ushered in. A very significant part of this weekly celebration consists of blessings bestowed upon family members and gratitude given to Adonai. As part of these blessings a mother or father will direct this specific blessing to the daughters of the home: Ye'simech Elohim ke-Sarah, Rivka, Ra-chel ve-Lay'ah. *May God make you like Sarah, Rebecca, Rachel and Leah.*

What characteristics do these Matriarchs have in common, and Leah possess in particular, that would merit such high honor? How have these women been woven into the fabric of our lives through their place in Jewish history? These women were all servants of God and as such give us great examples how He loves us in our own journeys.

Leah, most notably, found great favor as she gave birth to each of her sons and then named them according to how she viewed each birth as it reflected her relationship with Hashem (Hebrew for "The Name").

Leah, often thought of in reference to her "tender eyes" and her constant tears, was in fact one of the great female figures in Jewish history because of her place in the birth of the Jewish nation. Tears, however, are not always meant to draw pity. For Leah, tears may well have been the result of sadness at her predicament—her

lifelong yearning for the love of her husband—or they may have been tears of the Spirit. When we live in God's shadow and abide in His will, we will often find ourselves "teary-eyed." I have a dear friend who practically walks around with a box of tissues because every time she speaks her eyes well up. Her tears are genuine and this is a woman whose saintly countenance is almost visible. I am convinced that she is a modern day Leah. My friend's life isn't without heartache and pain; but they are not what is at the root of her tears. Her relationship with Christ is so all-consuming that tears are simply part and parcel of this woman's spirit.

So while we may feel sorry for Leah, I suggest that attitude would be incorrect. Even though she longed for the love of her husband, she was also given great blessings from God. In fact, it is for that reason—those great blessings—that Jewish homes today bless their daughters *to be like Leah.*

She was, after all, the mother of six of the sons from which the twelve tribes of Israel are formed. She was also the mother of two additional sons of Jacob through her maidservant, Zilpah. Leah is also the mother of Dinah, Jacob's daughter who is raped and whose rape is avenged by her brothers. In many ways her life appears to be a constant source of sadness and struggle and yet we see that ultimately Leah was both wife of Israel, for we know that Jacob, after his struggle with an angel, becomes known as the man Israel; and she was mother of nation of Israel as her last son, Judah, brought forth Judaism.

Leah is, then, correctly viewed as a powerful Matriarch of the faith. And as our Christian existence makes it ties to the Jewish faith, we are able to, as Christian women, look to Leah as a role model for many things. Christians are grafted into this heritage through their acceptance of Christ as Lord and Savior. Through this grafting, Christian women are able to look upon the Jewish Matriarchs for all the ways in which they teach us how to serve God. Leah's life serves as a model for the times we struggle to overcome our earthly woes

in order to live for God; to be Christ-like in our words and our actions regardless of our circumstances.

There are many views on Leah's "tender eyes" and yet, as I've indicated, it seems most apparent that her tender eyes, caused by years of weeping over a number of different things, might well be called "tears of the Spirit" or "holy tears." As Alice von Hildebrand might say, they indicate her "God-given sensitivity." It makes sense that Leah, considered a prophetess, would weep in her knowledge that the Spirit of God was calling upon her to participate in the creation of the Jewish nation and yet she could not reconcile this with the knowledge that her pre-arranged marriage was to be to Esau.

As a woman of great spiritual prowess Leah would have known from an early age that Esau was not cut out to be a patriarch of the faith. In fact, Leah would have understood, on a very deep level, that Jacob had usurped Esau's blessing in an almost righteous way. So her weeping would have been instigated by Rebekah's agreement, early on, with Laban (Rebekah's brother), that Esau and Jacob were intended for Leah and Rachel.

Knowing that she was being called to bring forth a Jewish nation, Leah's tears may have been tears of sorrow because her heart would have ached to participate in God's plan as she knew she supposed to do but knowing full well Esau's inability to take on such a role. It would not have been pity for herself; but, rather Leah would have agonized over not being able to participate in God's plan as she knew she was meant to do.

This, then, would also explain why Leah agreed to her father's infamously deceitful plan to give her to Jacob when Jacob had expected to be married to Rachel. It seems quite clear that Leah, while never abandoning her hope and desire to be loved by her husband, was willing to put aside her own wishes for happiness in order to fulfill the destiny to which she was called; a destiny fulfilled in her marriage to Jacob. At some point Jacob, too, must have

understood that God's call for Leah was to help bring forth a Jewish nation.

The birth of Leah's sons played a pivotal role in her place as Matriarch of the faith; as they gave rise to half of the twelve tribes of Israel. Leah's first son, Reuben, was the first born of all Jacob's children. God saw that Leah had boldly gone forth with His call on her life and rewarded her for her interior beauty that was found in her strength and spirit. While He kept Rachel's womb closed, He opened Leah's.

Genesis places much emphasis on Rachel's physical beauty but not on Leah's. Almost to the contrary we read about her "weak eyes." But it is in this physical lack that her inner beauty is able to shine. She helps us recognize that God does, in fact, look into our hearts.

Furthermore, the Jewish faith teaches that there are many blessings when one performs a good deed; a mitzvah. God would have looked, with favor, upon Leah's mitzvah of entering a loveless marriage to participate in God's plan for the birth of the Jewish nation.

God granted her the blessing of children. This first born, then, is recognition of the need and importance of performing good deeds for others and for the glory of God's kingdom. With Reuben's birth we also see Leah's continued hope that her husband will come to love her as she chooses the baby's name which, in essence, says: *Because Hashem has seen my humiliation, for my husband will now love me.* Unfortunately, this does not turn out to be the case and yet we will see from Leah's life that she continues to trust in God and live for His call upon her life.

Leah's second son is born and she also gives him a name that reflects her unending belief in God's graces. In many ways she simply refuses to believe that hope does not exist. She says, *Because Hashem has heard that I am not favored, He has given me this one also; and she called his name, Shimon.* Although the birth of this son does not bring Leah into the folds of Jacob's heart, nor satisfy her own

longings for love, we see that she continues to trust in God as she becomes pregnant with a third son. With his birth she says, *This time my husband will become attached to me because I have born him three sons; that is why she named him, Levi.* This son, Levi, begins the lineage of the Jewish priesthood; a mighty and powerful statement of how God blesses Leah.

Finally, Leah's forth son is born and named Judah. He is the father of the monarchy of Judaism and also plays an important role in the brothers' experience before Joseph in regards to Benjamin. Judah is also considered, by Leah, to be "more than her fair share of children" and recognizing the tremendous blessing from God for this fourth son she says, *This time I will praise the Lord.* With this birth Leah reveals how to move softly from faith, hope, and trust and into praise. What a beautiful lesson for us!

It is after the birth of Leah's four sons that she gives her maidservant to Jacob and two more sons are born before Leah, again, gives birth to the last three of her children: Issachar, Zeubulun, and Dinah.

Leah, along with Abraham, Isaac, Jacob, Sarah, and Rebekah, is buried in the Cave of Machpelah. She is, interestingly, buried next to Jacob. The Cave of Machpelah is considered to be the second holiest place in the Jewish faith after the Temple Mount in Jerusalem. Rachel is the only Matriarch to be buried elsewhere. She is buried near Bethlehem.

## *The Word of God*

*Those who sow in tears will reap with cries of joy. Those who go forth weeping, carrying sacks of seek, will return with cries of joy, carrying their bundled sheaves. Psalm 126:5-6*

*He has made everything beautiful in its time. He has also set eternity in the hearts of men; yet they cannot fathom what God has done from beginning to end. I know that there is nothing better for men than to be happy and do good while they live. That everyone may eat and drink, and find satisfaction in all his toil-this is the gift of God. Ecclesiastes 3:11-13*

*Come to me, all you who are weary and burdened, and I will give you rest. Take my yoke upon you and learn from me, for I am gentle and humble in hearts, and you will find rest for your souls. For my yoke is easy and my burden is light. Matthew 11:28-30*

*Finish this daughter's bridal week; then we will give you the younger one also, in return for another seven years of work. And Jacob did so. Genesis 29:27-28*

*Dear friends, if our hearts do not condemn us, we have confidence before God and receive from him anything we ask, because we obey his commands and do what pleases him. 1 John 3:21-22*

*Then he said, "May the Lord not be angry, but let me speak just once more. What if only ten can be found there?" He answered, "For the sake of ten, I will not destroy it [the city of Sodom]." When the Lord had finished speaking with Abraham, he left and Abraham returned home. Genesis 18:32-33*

*However, if you suffer as a Christian, do not be ashamed, but praise God that you bear that name. 1 Peter 4:1*

*Motherhood is the fruit of the marriage union of a man and woman, of that biblical "knowledge" which corresponds to the "union of the two in one flesh."*

Mulieris Dignitatem

## ***Shiphrah and Puah***

Before Pharaoh's daughter scoops Moses out of the Nile, Scripture introduces us to two Hebrew midwives. These women, Shiphrah and Puah, put their lives on the line in disobeying a directive from Pharaoh while ultimately being in obedience to God. They disregard Pharaoh's orders to kill all newborn Hebrew baby boys and in so doing teach us two wonderful aspects important to our roles as women of faith.

First, and foremost, these women teach us how to make our choices, regardless of consequences, based on the right fear of God. Recall that 'fear of the Lord' is a gift of the Holy Spirit. They teach us that fear of God is, in actuality, a fear of displeasing God. Fear of God is a right-placed knowledge that, in displeasing God, we jeopardize our relationship with Him. The fear comes from the realization of what our lives would be like without God.

Second, Shiphrah and Puah are examples of following the natural law that God placed in our heart. A law that connects us to God and exists in each and every one of us: a way that our conscience guides us and our spirit stays united to God. In disobeying Pharaoh's clear instructions, but following the natural law written in their hearts, these women live out the first and the sixth commandments, **prior** to Moses receiving them in written form.

The First Commandment, *"You shall have no other gods before Me,"* quite succinctly prioritizes our very existence. When it comes to rulers, authority, and the levels of any hierarchy, God trumps all. The idea that Shiphrah and Puah understand this before it exists in written form emphasizes the fact that there is a natural law, written upon our hearts, that draws us to God in all our circumstances. And, being guided by the Spirit, we are able to respond to that law, knowingly and without trepidation. Shiphrah and Puah give us a beautiful example of the natural law that forever tugs at us, pulling us towards God.

The Sixth Commandment, *"You shall not murder,"* also resides soundly in their hearts. We can look to Shiphrah and Puah as the first women to boldly live a pro-life message. And in living this message, which is pleasing to God, we find that they received blessings of their own. They made a difficult decision in the face of disobeying Pharaoh and yet stayed committed to their God, our God. When Pharaoh's edict came in conflict with their God's edict, as revealed to them in their hearts, they chose God.

More and more our secular lives are encroaching upon our Christian values and, like Shiphrah and Puah, we are in positions where we must take a stand. We should look to these women as heroines whose fear of displeasing God was the determining factor in the decisions they made.

Shiphrah and Puah faced two realities when they received the directive from Pharaoh to kill newborn Hebrew baby boys. They understood that one was a temporary reality while the other was an eternal reality. The first reality was to understand what would happen in disobeying Pharaoh. With this reality was the potential for severe or even life-or-death consequences. However, these wise women also understood that these consequences, regardless of their severity, were transitory. Let us recall, by meditating upon their actions, that wisdom is a gift of the Spirit and proceeds from fear of the Lord.

The second reality these women understood was the necessity of obeying God. Shiphrah and Puah were not willing to disobey the God they served. For them, the everlasting consequences of this must have far outweighed the temporal consequences of disobeying Pharaoh. So, in a few short verses we see two women using their free will in a noble and profound way. We see two women taking the first pro-life stand in the book of Exodus.

Undoubtedly current secularism makes us face our pro-life commitments in uncomfortable and often unpopular ways. However, like Shiphrah and Puah, we too must take a stand. We, too, must witness to the value of each human life. We must also respond to the natural law written in our hearts in which God reminds us that He determines the beginning and end of each of our lives. We are called to work with Him in all aspects of life knowing that He will, one day, welcome us home with open arms. And on that day we will give an accounting of our life on earth. We want that accounting to be pleasing to Him and without regrets.

After we learn that Shiphrah and Puah disobey Pharaoh to obey God, their brief story ends in the simplest of lines. We read…*And because the midwives feared God, he gave them families of their own.* No fanfare, just a fundamental recognition of the favor we find with God when we choose to do His work. Often the favor includes earthly benefits but always the favor includes heavenly blessings.

Current medical, technological, and scientific advances have made it imperative that we understand what the Catholic Church teaches on life issues. According to The Center for Bio-Ethical Reform, 1.37 million abortions are performed each year with over 30% performed on Catholic women. Only 1% of all abortions are said to occur because of rape or incest and 6% due to health problems for the mother and/or child.

What began as a way to legalize an unsafe but supposedly "necessary" medical procedure has gotten out of control. The Catholic Church teaches that abortion is intrinsically evil and yet,

according to Zenit.org, more than half of American Catholics voted for Barack Obama in the 2008 presidential race in which the candidate clearly stated his pro-death stance.

We live at a time where the capabilities of the medical establishment, and so many other organizations, are far beyond what our sisters-in-faith could have ever fathomed. "*It is quite conceivable that the mind-boggling technological progress of the last sixty years, if severed from wisdom, will bring about man's downfall*," writes von Hildebrand.

Clearly, then, Shiphrah and Puah were women with wisdom and courage.

Let us be inspired by Shiphrah and Puah's example of pro-life decisions, in obedience to the awesome God that we serve, knowing that our rewards come in eternal packages. Let us not contribute to the downfall of man; but, rather, let us build up the world in which we live by honoring the dignity of every unborn child and understand all the ways in which we can honor life.

Alice von Hildebrand powerfully states:

*One day, all human accomplishments will be reduced to a pile of ashes. But every single child to whom a woman has given birth will live forever, for he has been given an immortal soul made to God's image and likeness.*

Such words as von Hildebrand's remind us of the power we have as women, both in the choosing of life but also in the ways we uphold it as intrinsically valuable. Indeed, we are quite fortunate because we are able to speak in a multitude of ways. Women speak through the values they impart to their children and how they spend their time. They speak through the dollars they spend and the shows they watch. Women speak through their vote and through the alliances they maintain.

Shiphrah and Puah, whose mention is so fleeting in Exodus, remind us that our lives, too, are just as fleeting and the stands we take are just as important. They show us that all the legislation written, passed, and amended will not replace the natural law that God lovingly placed within our hearts.

## *The Word of God*

*I urge you, brothers, to watch out for those who cause divisions and put obstacles in your way that are contrary to the teaching you have learned. Keep away from them. Romans 16:17*

*You shall not murder. Genesis 20:13*

*The mind of a sinful man is death, but the mind controlled by the Spirit is life and peace. Romans 8:6*

*The king of Egypt said to the Hebrew midwives, whose names were Shiphrah and Puah, "When you help the Hebrew women in childbirth and observe them on the delivery stool, if it is a boy, kill him; but if it is a girl, let her live," The midwives, however feared God and did not do what the king of Egypt had told them to do; they let the boys live...So God was kind to the midwives and the people increased and became even more numerous. And because the midwives feared God, he gave them families of their own. Exodus 1:15-21*

*We wait in hope for the Lord; he is our help and our shield. In him our hearts rejoice, for we trust in his holy name. Psalm 33:20-21*

*Have no anxiety at all, but in everything, by prayer and petition, with thanksgiving, make your requests known to God. Then the peace of God that surpasses all understanding will guard your hearts and mind in Christ Jesus. Philippians 4:6-7*

*Those controlled by the sinful nature cannot please God. You, however, are controlled not by the sinful nature but by the Spirit, if the Spirit of God lives in you. Romans 8:8-9*

*Created in the image and likeness of God as a "unity of the two," both have been called to a spousal love.*

Mulieris Dignitatem

## *Zipporah*

Like so many other women in our world, we know about Zipporah through the success of her husband. Of course, not many of our husbands have such name recognition as Moses, but the story is the same. Oftentimes we find ourselves in the background, nurturing our friends, our spouses, our children, and our neighbors. And, like Zipporah, we have a name and a commitment to the ones we love but it isn't necessarily our name that the world or the community might know. Or our role is diminished because it is the less sought after role of homemaker or mother. Fortunately for us, the Lord will know the fruits of our love. He will recognize our dedication to those in He put in our lives and in our corner of the world.

Scripture gives us role models for nurturers as well as for prophetesses and judges. We see women summoned by God in numerous ways. And regardless of the summons, God's hand is evident in the uniqueness of each and every call. Of course the secular messages aren't always as evident. We often struggle to find our place, as defined by the world. However, when we are guided by the Holy Spirit we are able to cut through the cloudiness of the secular messages that are, at once, loud and yet contradictory.

We have all in one way or another experienced the haziness of the world's messages. We might even have found it difficult to be at peace with what feels "right" because we are often told that it is "wrong." If we are at home, raising children, the world tells us that

we will miss opportunities in our careers. If we choose our careers society tells us that we will miss our child's first steps and first words. If we remain childless the world tells us that we are selfish. If we have six children we are treated as if we are irresponsible. The tumultuousness of the messages takes its toll.

When we find ourselves in the midst of this, it is crucial to bring our focus back to God. When we surrender our lives to Him, He can work with us as He sees fit: not as the world tells us, nor as our false sense of "truth" tells us.

Zipporah, then, is the great reminder that God's plans are often in absolute contrast to what we might have planned or what we might be told is "right." And she then shows us how to gracefully accept what the Lord puts on our plate. Most certainly her life unfolded in a way that was in stark contrast to what she would have imagined. We ought to find great faith in that simple realization. From it we can clearly see that the Lord always knows what is best for each and every one of us and willingly looks to work with us to that end.

It would seem safe to say that while Zipporah was tending to sheep and found the stranger, Moses, at the well, she did not conceive of what lay ahead. Could she have fathomed, even for an instant, that this man would soon be her husband and in direct communication with God—talking to a burning bush and receiving commandments? If she imagined herself as a wife and mother it would, no doubt, have been in very conventional ways. But her resolve to love and support her husband allowed God's plan to unfold. And, as it turned out, it was a very unconventional, complex plan which included parting a huge body of water and multiple plagues! So when Zipporah participated in God's plans, she was able to be all that God hoped for and needed her to be.

In a very trusting and loving way, Zipporah went along with the life that was developing. She shows us that her part in Exodus was as valuable to God's plans as was Moses receiving the Ten Commandments and parting the Red Sea. After all, had she wanted

to make things difficult for Moses, we all know she could have. She could have, like Eve, forever changed the course of human history.

Instead she relied on her confidence as a wife, mother, and woman. She was not affected by the realization that her life, her marriage, was anything other than what she had probably dreamt about. In Moses' life Zipporah was the perfect complement to his mother. Herself a woman whose faith in God allowed her to release Moses into the Nile. When we meditate on the women in Moses' life, it is no wonder that he was able to build the most loving of relationships with God. He was himself blessed with women in his life who were resolute in their faith. These women were able to turn everything over to God, fully trusting in His omniscience.

Zipporah's everyday life shows us that she was strong, loving, and faithful. She was both self-confident and self-effacing at the same time. She had to be all these things, and more, to live a life outside of the normal expectations as her husband moved forward in God's plan for the Hebrew people. She was a mighty and powerful woman. Consider, even for a brief moment, how accomplishing her role also allowed Moses to reach his destiny for God and ultimately scribe the Torah. God came upon Moses during the return to Egypt and would have killed Moses had it not been for Zipporah's quick understanding that their son needed to be circumcised and, taking a piece of flint, performing the circumcision herself.

It is both illuminating and exhilarating for those of us in positions to offer nurturing and support to others. It inspires us to embrace the opportunities that the Holy Spirit gives us in which we can help one another in our walk with God. We learn that no task is too large or small for us to handle.

We should all recognize that as women we have the same influencing power that Zipporah possessed. So if our life is one of nurturing and support, and it is dismissed, we should recall how Zipporah's nurturing love allowed Moses to free God's people. Whatever she did on the "home-front" allowed Moses to

wholeheartedly tend to God's people. It was in that supportive way that she had an enormous effect on a multitude of people.

We see from Zipporah that a woman who loves and encourages her spouse, her children, or her friends is actually able to impact a tremendous amount of people. It literally becomes her character that moves out into the world through these people. Her kindness and her compassion are able to take on a life of their own. A woman's influence, and her subsequent responsibility, should never be underestimated.

And, of course, the opposite is true. A difficult, angry, unkind woman just as easily sends negative or detrimental energy out into the world. Our behavior always has an effect on others. At the end of our lives we will come face to face with God. We will be held responsible for our words and our actions. It will be at that point that the realization of how we treated others will most fully impact us. We will learn how we have affected others' lives. We will be held accountable. We would do well, then, to learn from Zipporah the intrinsic value of creating a loving, supportive home.

Make no mistake about it; women are very powerful creatures. How we use that power—that feminine genius—is of our own choosing. Do we, like Zipporah, allow God's plan to unfold, especially if it is different than we had imagined? Do we trust God and the path that He has put us on? Or do we hinder Him in untold ways? Are we brave enough, like Zipporah, to find our worth in a solid marriage or do we let others shake our foundation?

Consider King David's wife Abigail, a woman very much like Zipporah, powerfully imbued with the Spirit of God. As David's third wife, she was the one who brought to David a harmony he had not yet experienced. Abigail intercepted David as he was on his way to kill her first husband, himself apparently a greedy, stupid man who refused to reciprocate David's guardianship over land and animals. Right away we see that Abigail is able to grasp the seriousness of the situation that eluded her husband and in that way

spared his life from David's impending plan. This is similar to Zipporah saving Moses' life when God was out to kill him (Exodus 4:24-26). We read that Zipporah, imbued with the Spirit, understood the ways of God and stepped in to keep Moses from harm.

Just so, Abigail knew immediately upon approaching David that she was in the presence of greatness from God and bowed to show her respect and understanding. While David went on to have many more wives, it is Abigail who brought the balance into David's life that most assuredly allowed him to continue with his own predestination.

Zipporah's beautiful story, as well as the story of Abigail, is one of trust and courage for married women. Both women reflect that in the Spirit a woman is powerful and resilient. Both encourage us to face the secular skepticism that says we cannot be fully happy or complete in a mutually respectful relationship. Both women show us how to trust our mates and how to trust God.

Zipporah, then, gives us the courage to stand firm when the world tells us to fold. She is a woman whose powerful ability to offer nurturing love and support to a man on a treacherous mission ultimately allowed God's plan for His people to be realized. Abigail, too, reflects what a woman is able to bring to a man and to a home: harmony, nurturance, and stability. These are things to value and uphold. They are things of God and are God-honoring.

God would have known, as His word indicates in Genesis 2:24, that in choosing Moses, He was also choosing Zipporah. She was a woman, like Noah's wife, up to the great task ahead. Like Abigail, Zipporah is truly a woman for all times as she embodies strength, fortitude, and trust. Zipporah, Abigail, Noah's wife; All strong women whose lives illustrate a woman's ability to affect the world from within the walls of her home, from her daily living in the Spirit of God.

## *The Word of God*

*For this reason a man will leave his father and mother and be united to his wife, and they will become one flesh. Genesis 2:24*

*Husbands, love your wives, just as Christ loved the church...In this same way, husbands ought to love their wives as their own bodies. He who loves his wife loves himself...However each of you also must love his wife as he loves himself, and the wife must respect her husband. Ephesians 5:25-33*

*When one finds a worthy wife her value is far beyond pearls. Proverbs 31:10*

*And where is he? He asked his daughters, "Why did you leave him? Invite him to have something to eat." Moses agreed to stay with the man, who gave his daughter Zipporah to Moses in marriage. Zipporah gave birth to a son, and Moses named him Gershom, saying, "I have become an alien in a foreign land." Exodus 2:20-22*

*On the journey, at a place where they spent the night, the Lord came upon Moses and would have killed him. But Zipporah took a piece of flint and cut off her son's foreskin and, touching his person, she said, "You are a spouse of blood to me." Then God let Moses go. Exodus 4:24-25*

*She [the ideal wife] is clothed with strength and dignity, and she laughs at the days to come. She opens her mouth in wisdom, and on her tongue is kindly counsel. Proverbs 31:25-26*

*David said to Abigail: Blessed be the Lord, the God of Israel, who sent you to meet me today. Blessed be your good judgment and blessed be you yourself, who this day have prevented me from shedding blood and from avenging myself personally...1 Samuel 25:32-33*

*In the Spirit of Christ, in fact, women can discover the entire meaning of their femininity and thus be disposed to making a "sincere gift of self" to others, thereby finding themselves.*

Mulieris Dignitatem

### *Miriam*

Miriam's life, as older sister of Moses, is quite interesting. As a young seven-year-old girl, she places her infant brother into a basket and then places that basket into the Nile where, hiding in the reeds, she watches as he is found by Pharaoh's daughter. From there this incredibly brave little girl offers Pharaoh's daughter a nursemaid for this newly found infant; the nursemaid, of course, being Moses' mother. With the great plans that God has in store for Moses, we should not be surprised at the women to whom he was given care: women whose presence in his life, at critical junctures, created an environment for him to answer God; women whose very presence safeguarded his life when it might have otherwise been lost.

He was born of a humble servant, a Hebrew woman whose faith in God allowed her to place her newborn son in a basket to be floated down the Nile. He was given a sister whose bravery belied her young age and who rose to be a significant force in the freeing of the Hebrew slaves. Finally, Moses marries an Ethiopian woman, Zipporah, whose acceptance of her husband's call allows Moses to fulfill God's plan most successfully.

Miriam grows from a young child who played a critical role in the survival of Moses to a young woman, referred to as the first prophetess of the Hebrew people. Hundreds of years after Miriam's

death, the prophet Micah reminded the Hebrews that three people freed them from slavery: Moses, Aaron, and Miriam. This is quite a significant recognition given to her. We also know that, during this event in which Micah gives Miriam equal credit for releasing the Israelites from Egyptian slavery; Miriam was a formidable presence whose song of praise to God greatly inspired the Hebrew women. In all aspects of her life Miriam moved with God, just as her younger brother did.

Maybe that is why, when she and Aaron let the fruits of their spirit become mired in envy, God chose a swift punishment for her: leprosy. Prior to the exchange in which Miriam and Aaron questioned Moses being the only recipient of God's words, Miriam consistently produced the fruits by which Christ said we would be known: love, joy, peace, longsuffering, gentleness, goodness, faith, meekness and temperance.

Until that time, Miriam had lovingly and joyfully served God, who reciprocally elevated her to the same status as Aaron. Her countenance was one of peace and longsuffering for her people. Her goodness was evident in her life as a young child following her mother's wishes and safeguarding her brother. So when she let her envy cloud her judgment and fell prey to "bad-mouthing" God's most humble servant, Moses, God's punishment was speedy and without regard to her status. In that, we see that our own journey's are always under the scrutiny of the laws set down by Christ. We are called to produce the fruits of the Spirit in ways that our lives reflect Christ's working within us.

As we would imagine, Moses does plead to God for Miriam's healing and it is given. However, as we serve a righteous God, we see that Miriam must still suffer consequences for her actions and she is dispelled from her community for seven days. The message: God is a just God, even to those who most faithfully serve Him. Does He not withhold Moses from entering the Promised Land? He does. And we know that no one was ever more loved than Moses to whom God admittedly spoke face-to-face.

Should this fact frighten us or deter us from our lifelong quest of perseverance for the race set before us? It should not. From the tender age of seven, we see that Miriam's life was truly a "lifelong" journey.

We learn from Miriam that even on our most graced days, we are often tempted to be less than Christian. Even when we are surrounded by God's mercy and blessings, we must rise above the secular circumstances in which we live. While some of our battles will be easily won, others will require intercession. We may rely on our friends and family for aid in an earthly manner or for spiritual help in the way of prayers.

And the opposite is true as well. We are called to help others in their journey: whether through intercessory prayer or with earthly support in difficult and trying circumstances. Miriam's life is also a reflection on the joy and inspiration we can supply to others. As Christians we rely heavily upon community; both as participants and as recipients. God has always called us to be in community, knowing that we each possess different gifts that glorify His kingdom; all necessary and equally important.

Ultimately, Miriam's life emphasizes how God calls each of us to work within our own circumstances for His kingdom and to recognize our total and complete reliance on Him as sovereign Lord and Creator. With Him we are able to do everything. Without Him we are as helpless as newborn babes.

# *The Word of God*

*He who guards his mouth protects his life; to open wide one's lips brings downfall. Proverbs 13:3*

*For I brought you up from the land of Egypt, from the place of slavery I released you; And I sent you Moses, Aaron, and Miriam. Micah 6:4*

*His sister stationed herself at a distance to find out what would happen to him. Exodus 2:4*

*He said to his disciples, "Things that cause sin will inevitably occur, but woe to the person through whom they occur. Luke 17:1*

*Then his sister asked Pharaoh's daughter, "Shall I go and call one of the Hebrew women to nurse the child for you?" Exodus 3:7*

*The prophetess Miriam, Aaron's sister, took a tambourine in her hands, while all the women went out after her with tambourines, dancing; and she led them in the refrain: Sing to the Lord, for he is gloriously triumphant; horse and chariot he has cast into the sea. Exodus 15:20-21*

*Finally, brothers, rejoice. Mend your ways, encourage one another, agree with one another, live in peace, and the God of love and peace will be with you. 2 Corinthians 13:11*

*The Church gives thanks for all the manifestations of the feminine "genius" which have appeared in the course of history, in the midst of all peoples and nations; she gives thanks for all the charisms which the Holy Spirit distributes to women in the history of the People of God, for all the victories which she owes to their faith, hope and charity: she gives thanks for all the fruits of feminine holiness.*

Mulieris Dignitatem

## *Deborah*

Understanding the story of Deborah, a prophetess and judge, begins with a general understanding of the history of God's people, the Israelites. Deborah, like many of the women in our faith history, was herself Jewish. She ruled over God's people with fairness and insight.

From the time of Genesis, in which God created Adam and Eve, to the time of Deborah, the people of God had been in and out of His favor numerous times. During these tumultuous times they both angered Him as well as cried out to Him for deliverance. From chapter three in Judges to chapter four in Judges we hear three different instances when the Israelites offended God, fell under the power of a foreign ruler, and then cried out to God for help and forgiveness. It has been said that, as a result of each of these upheavals, the Hebrew people drew closer to God.

Nonetheless, at the time of Deborah we find that the Israelites had again offended God and were being oppressed by a Canaanite king whose army was under the rule of General Sisera. Judges had been governing the Israelites who, unlike any neighboring nations, recognized the one true God. These judges, like Deborah, had the

respect due their position. People would take their troubles and disagreements to the judge. The judge would administer rulings, admonishments, and consequences. For the Israelite people, God was king but there was still a need for earthly jurisprudence. That was the role and responsibility of the judges: to maintain civility and equity among the people. For many years this was the way in which the Hebrew people conducted their daily affairs.

Deborah's beautiful story shows us how God will call women to all positions and walks in life. He determines who is best suited in a particular set of circumstances. It is then our responsibility to fill our role with the Scripture characteristics that are held in high esteem: perseverance, joy, gratitude, and wisdom among others. Deborah, herself, would have been a role model for characteristics that the Lord values.

She would have embodied the traits necessary to be a judge for the Jewish people. In that role, the traits would have particularly included strength, wisdom, and wealth. But we would not understand the meaning of these traits by applying today's definitions. Just like we often misunderstand the meaning of humility when serving the Lord, we would probably misunderstand the meanings implied by these adjectives as well.

For instance, Deborah's strength would have been reflected in her ability to conquer her natural desires. As we learn from Eve, succumbing to temptation is much easier than walking away from it. And yet, this is what we must train ourselves to do. So Deborah would have displayed an ability to overcome the desires of the flesh and to walk more fully in the Spirit. As we know, this doesn't happen without a deep and trusting relationship with God. We can assume that her relationship with the Father would have given her the strength needed in her earthly walk to overcome the temptations in her life.

There is a saying that a smart man learns from his own mistakes and a wise man learns from the mistakes of others. This is how Deborah

would have shown her wisdom. She would have learned from others' mistakes and applied those understandings to situations in her community. As a judge she would have been able to administer justice based upon the experiences of those around her. She would have been able to take lessons learned from one set of circumstances and apply them to other circumstances. And, in so doing, she showed the true meaning of wisdom. Scripture is replete with our call to gain wisdom and Deborah would have been considered "wise" to be called to such a position in her life.

The third characteristic that Deborah would have embodied was wealth. But her wealth would have been evident in her satisfaction with life and an accompanying inner peace. We can assume that instead of complaining about a long "work" day or the petty grievances that she had to hear, she must have begun and ended each day with a gratitude for what it would hold or held. Our world is filled with sagas of greed and treachery. We know from these stories that material wealth does not satisfy the soul. This is why wealth, by Old Testament standards, refers to an inner peace. It is that same inner peace that Jesus left to us. He knew that inner peace was true wealth. And in that way, Deborah was deemed quite wealthy.

Deborah, then, embodies characteristics that God would like us to manifest as well. She was wealthy because of her gratitude for the life that the Lord gave her. She was wise as she continuously applied newly acquired knowledge to a variety of situations. And she was strong in her ability to be guided by the Spirit and to resist the temptations of life. Deborah helps us understand how we can better serve God when we embrace and develop these anointed traits in our own lives. She was qualified to be both a prophetess and judge for the Jewish people. And in that role she was able to bring God's people out from oppression.

As a prophetess and judge Deborah is able to deliver the news of how God's people will be delivered from the tyrannical Canaanite king. Deborah shares this plan with the commander of the Israelite

army. In sharing God's plan with the commander, we immediately witness the commander's great dependence on her. He says, *"If you come with me, I will go; if you do not come with me, I will not go."* It seems odd to hear a mighty General saying such things to a woman. Odder yet is her response. In it we recognize her great dependence and trust in God. Recall that, as a prophetess, she was simply revealing God's plan to the General. As such she easily knew her trust in God was well placed and was able to reply saying, *"I will certainly go with you."* She then adds that, although they will have success, the Canaanite General will fall not to the Israelite commander but to a woman. Again a simple sharing of God's plan with no self-aggrandizing attached: strong in following the Spirit, wise in learning from those around her, and wealthy in accepting this role.

In this decisive exchange we see the courage that women must often have in fulfilling their purpose. We also see the extent to which others, even those in great and powerful positions, rely on women. Deborah epitomizes the strength and courage women possess in all walks of life. She shows us that when we are in compliance with God's will, we help make the impossible become possible. Deborah, then, will go with the Israelite commander and conquer the Canaanite army but the Canaanite General, Sisera, will not be conquered in this battle. He will fall to a woman.

True to His word, as delivered through Deborah, God brought the entire Canaanite army down. General Sisera, as expected, escaped. He fled to the tent of Jael, the wife of an ally. Again, as Deborah had prophesized, Sisera fell to a woman: to Jael. With Sisera asleep in her tent, Jael murdered him. With the death of the Canaanite General, and the subsequent humiliation to the Canaanite King, came freedom to the Israelites. From this point we learn that the land had peace for forty years.

There are so many aspects of Deborah's personality that speaks to women of today. She was a respected leader, prophetess, and judge. She showed great trust in the plan that God shared with her and tremendous courage in a very difficult time. She had great Generals acquiesce to her authority and was both open and honest in her conduct. Deborah is a beautiful heroine. Her self-assurance is worthy of respect and admiration. Although it would be foolish to imagine that she was without her qualms, she shows us that her confidence and trust in God makes all things possible. And, reciprocally, God was able to work with Deborah because of her humility, faith, and obedience.

Like Deborah, we too, are able to listen to God in our lives. We are right to assume that He would like to guide us, through His spirit, in ways that we might never imagine. We know that He works all things for His good and we would do well to move forward with the understanding that our role in His plan is both vital and necessary. Just as Deborah accomplished great things for God, we too can accomplish great things for God.

We also have to be fascinated by the role that Jael plays in the fall of the Canaanite General. Here is a woman whose mention, although minor, plays a major role in the history of God's people. Recall that Deborah told the Israelite commander that Sisera, the Canaanite General, would fall to a woman. What a potent statement: the fact that the Israelite army would defeat the entire Canaanite army and yet the Canaanite General, the top man, would fall to a woman. And in Sisera's demise was the ultimate demise of the Canaanites, brought about by a woman following God's call on her life.

When we are given the opportunity to show our might and strength in God, do we heed His call? As Disciples of Christ, we are all called for a unique and worthy purpose. We are all placed within a particular set of circumstances, interacting with a given group of friends and acquaintances. Our unique paths allow us to proclaim our faith in both words and deeds. We are, on the one hand, living in a time where worshiping God is neither accepted nor embraced. On the other hand we are also seeing a spread of Christianity to the ends of the earth. It is an interesting situation. We can certainly rest assured that we have a role to play that will help God's plan for

humanity to unfold. And so, like Deborah, God calls each of us to be strong and faithful to Him.

Trusting in His providence, learning His word, and inviting His active participation in our lives makes our relationship with God vibrant and strong. It is in that symbiotic relationship that we can be called to do His will. He guides, we move; we talk, He listens. Over time the exchanges between our Creator and ourselves becomes quite fluid. A synchronicity begins to develop that is both pleasing to God and fulfilling to us. We are walking with Him and begin to fully understand such terms as "fear of the Lord." In connecting with Him our fear is to face a time when we would be without Him. And so, we begin to care more about our relationship with Him than ever before. Like Deborah and Jael before us, we recognize our complete dependence on Him.

Deborah's life, then, is testimony to the great call God has in store for us and our friends and family. Each and every one of us has that unique part to fill; that reason we exist. All pieces, regardless of the worldly view, are critical to God's plan. So, whether we are warriors or judges, whether we are mothers or advocates, our destiny is our own. And God looks for us to fill it with vigor and joy.

Our destiny is our own

*In the same way, the Spirit helps us in our weakness. We do not know what we ought to pray for, but the Spirit himself intercedes for us with groans that words cannot express. And he who searches our hearts knows the mind of the Spirit, because the Spirit intercedes for the saints in accordance with God's will. Romans 8:26-27*

*Rejoice in the Lord always. I shall say it again: rejoice! Your kindness should be known to all. The Lord is near. Philippians 4:4-5*

*Deborah, a prophetess, the wife of Lappidoth, was leading Israel at that time. She held court under the Palm of Deborah between Ramah and Bethel in the hill country of Ephraim, and the Israelites came to her to have their disputes decided. Judges 4:4-5*

*Sisera, however, fled on foot to the tent of Jael, the wife of Heber the Kenite, because there were friendly relations between Jabin, king of Hazor and the clan of Heber the Kenite. Judges 4:17*

*Listen to me, you who pursue justice, who seek the Lord; Look to the rock from which you were hewn, to the pit from which you were quarried; Look to Abraham, your father, and to Sarah, who gave you birth; When he was but one I called him, I blessed him and made him many; Yes, the Lord shall comfort Zion and have pity on her ruins; Her deserts he shall make like Eden; her wasteland like the garden of the Lord; Joy and gladness shall be found in her, thanksgiving and the sound of song. Isaiah 51:1-3*

*For this we toil and struggle, because we have set our hope on the living God, who is the savior of all, especially of those who believe. 1 Timothy 4:10*

*It was not through law that Abraham and his offspring received the promise that he would be heir of the world, but through the righteousness that comes by faith. Romans 4:13*

*Every vocation has a profoundly personal and prophetic meaning.*

Mulieris Dignitatem

## *Ruth*

Ruth is a Moabite who came to be a daughter-in-law of Naomi, a Hebrew woman. Naomi and her husband, along with their two sons, were forced to leave their town of Bethlehem due to a famine. They traveled to Moab where Elimelech, Naomi's husband, soon died. In Moab, Ruth's sons married Moabite women. One son married Orpah and the other married Ruth. After a decade or so, Naomi's sons also died, leaving Naomi without a husband or children but with two daughters-in-law.

Hearing that the Lord had provided food for the people of Bethlehem, Naomi decided to move back to her home in Bethlehem. She encouraged her daughters-in-law to move on with their lives. Naomi fully expected Orpah and Ruth to stay in Moab and remarry. She must have been a bit taken aback when she heard Ruth's response.

While Orpah agrees to go her own way and sadly says her "good-byes" to Naomi, Ruth refuses to part. She makes the bold claim that nothing but death will separate her from Naomi and Naomi's God. At this point Naomi sees that it would be futile to try to persuade Ruth to stay behind. This must touch Naomi's heart in a way that we can only imagine. Although Naomi had lost her husband and her two sons, she was given the love of family in Ruth.

When we consider that Ruth cannot fathom leaving Naomi, we have to be in awe of what a loving woman Naomi must have been. Certainly we can assume that Naomi was a powerful witness to the Lord and that Ruth's heart was fertile ground for such a message. We are once again reminded how our actions are always affecting others. We are forced to ask ourselves some very powerful questions.

For instance, are we living in such a way that our life is a testimony to our faith? If God puts someone in our life whose heart is fertile ground for the Word, are we sowing potential seeds? The relationship between Naomi and Ruth prompts us to ask tough questions of ourselves, remembering that witnessing to those who share our faith is easy but being able to witness to those outside of our faith is another story. Are we sowing, through words and deeds, in the places that God wants?

As we continue to read the story of Ruth we hear Naomi soon refer to Ruth as her "daughter." She becomes an "adopted" child. Ruth is enfolded into Naomi's life in such a way that the foreshadowing of Gentiles being enfolded into the message of Jesus is quite evident. Ruth, an "outsider," represents the Gentiles who were originally "outsiders" to the Good News. Remember that Ruth is purposely, and with her free will, choosing Naomi's God to call her own. Just as we purposely, and with free will, accept Jesus.

Indeed, Ruth's story is filled with the foreshadowing of our own salvation: her story is one of commitment, redemption, and the lineage of Jesus Christ. Through Ruth we understand what the Lord requires of us to be in His favor: a deep abiding love and free acceptance. Ruth, in both her words and her actions, is a clear and concise example of commitment and love. Her love for Naomi, and subsequently Naomi's God, is what motivates her to leave her old life behind and stay with Naomi. It reminds us that we are all called to witness to the potential "Ruths" in our lives.

We are all called to be beacons of light to others. So, just as Naomi's countenance was able to draw Ruth to the God of the Hebrew people, so our countenance should be such as to draw non-believers or tepid followers more closely into the fold that Jesus offers. Additionally we see that Ruth quite willingly leaves her home and possessions behind. In doing that, Ruth continues to model for us a behavior pleasing to Jesus.

This is, in fact, exactly what Jesus requires of us, His disciples. Whatever we know our earthly attachments to be, Jesus calls us to be able to leave them behind. He promises us that, in so doing, our lives will be in keeping with the Father's will. And then, and only then, can we inherit the kingdom of heaven. Our love for Jesus is shown in our everyday words and actions, just as Ruth's love for Naomi and Naomi's God is shown through her everyday words and actions.

We all know that it is fairly easy to make a claim of discipleship. Ruth gives us the courage to make the claim and, as is often said, "walk the talk." Ruth is a beautiful example of witnessing.

Ruth's story continues as she and Naomi move to Bethlehem. Ruth then, living in the town of Bethlehem, finds herself in a position to be the recipient of extreme kindness from a man named Boaz. In Ruth's story we learn of the practice of "redemption." Essentially this custom allows a close relative of a deceased man the option to take care of, or marry, a family member, thus carrying on the family line and "salvaging" or "redeeming" the family name. Boaz was a relative of Elimelech and exercised that option to marry Ruth, Elimelech's daughter-in-law.

With this act comes the true story of our redemption through Christ. Like Ruth, we were "outsiders" to the covenant. And yet we have also been redeemed, just as Ruth was, through Christ's great love for each and every one of us.

With Ruth's marriage to Boaz, another critical piece to our faith-life is put in place. Ruth becomes pregnant and gives birth to Obed. Obed was the father of Jesse, who was the father of David. David, we know is the line from which our Savior will be born. With Ruth's redemption we again witness God's love and His hand in all the lives of those that love and follow Him.

Ruth's story is both simple and yet quite complex. Through her innocent act of love towards her mother-in-law she becomes integral to the family line that will ultimately bring salvation. She teaches us the beauty of a love so pure that it cannot escape the imprint of God: a love that we are called to imitate and bring forth into the world.

# *The Word of God*

*Anyone who loves his father or mother more than me is not worthy of me; anyone who loves his son or daughter more than me is not worthy of me; and anyone who does not take his cross and follow me is not worthy of me. Whoever finds his life will lose it, and whoever loses his life for my sake will find it. Matthew 10:37-39*

*When the Almighty was yet with me, and my children were round about me; When my footsteps were bathed in milk, and the rock flowed with streams of oil; When I went forth to the gate of the city and set up my seat in the square—Then the young men saw me and withdrew while the elders rose up and stood; The chief men refrained from speaking and covered their moths with their hands; The voice of the princes was silenced, and their tongues stuck to the roofs of their mouths. Job 29:5-10*

*Remember your Creator in the days of your youth, before the evil days come and the years approach of which you will say, I have no pleasure in them; Before the sun is darkened, and the light, and the moon, and the stars, while the clouds return after the rain. Song of Songs 12:1-2*

*Realize then that it is those who have faith who are children of Abraham. Scripture, which saw in advance that God would justify the Gentiles by faith, foretold the good news to Abraham saying, "Through you shall all the nations be blessed." Consequently, those who have faith are blessed along with Abraham who had faith. For all who depend on works of the law are under a curse; for it is written, "Cursed be everyone who does not persevere in doing all the things written in the book of the law." Galatians 3:7-10*

*Then David gave his son Solomon the pattern of the portico and of the building itself, with its storerooms, its upper rooms and inner chambers, and the room with the propitiatory. 1 Chronicles 28:11*

*Then the women said to Naomi, "Blessed is the Lord who has not failed to provide you today with an Heir! May he become famous in Israel! Ruth 4:14*

*And may the Lord make you increase and abound in love for one another and for all, just as we have for you, 1 Thessalonians 3:1*

*But Ruth replied, "Don't urge me to leave you or to turn back from you. Where you go I will go, and where you stay I will stay. Your people will be my people and your God my God. Where you die I will die, and there I will be buried. May the Lord deal with me, be it ever so severely, if anything but death separates you and me. When Naomi realized that Ruth was determined to go with her, she stopped urging her. Ruth 1:16-18*

*But he entered the Most Holy Place once for all by his own blood, having obtained eternal redemption. Hebrews 9:12b*

*Trust in the Lord, your God, and you will be found firm. Trust in his prophets and you will succeed. 2 Chronicles 20:20b*

*A human being, whether male or female, is a person, and therefore, "the only creature on earth which God willed for its own sake;" and at the same time this unique and unrepeatable creature "cannot fully find himself except through the sincere gift of self."*

**Mulieris Dignitatem**

## *Esther*

*Dispatches were sent by couriers to all the king's provinces with the order to destroy, kill and annihilate all the Jews-young and old, women and little children-on a single day, the thirteenth day of the twelfth month, the month of Adar, and to plunder their goods.* Esther 3:13.

And so it was that Queen Esther found herself in a situation where she was able to bring about the rescue of God's people, the Jews. Esther had been made queen after Queen Vashti disobeyed orders and was removed from her throne. During the process to fill Queen Vashti's position, Esther's Jewish identify was never revealed. But it is her Jewish identify that would play a significant role in her future as queen.

Esther is called upon by her caretaker, Mordecai, to use her position and approach the king regarding the plan against the Jews. At first Esther's response is hesitant but she soon becomes receptive and pours herself wholeheartedly into the task at hand. Esther was, like so many of us have been, in the right place at the right time. And although we may not always recognize God's hand in things, it is there nonetheless.

Our lesson from Esther is in seeing how she most assuredly knew how to proceed. She shows us how to move productively in the situations in which God puts us, relying on our faith in Him.

Through God's providence Esther became queen and had a role to fill, a purpose to serve. We can certainly see how God's hand was in the details that moved Esther into her position to replace Queen Vashti.

It all began when Queen Vashti disobeyed the king's order to appear before the court. Her disobedience was seen as a possible precedent for other people to disobey the king and so she was removed from her position. It was then suggested that the king *give her royal position to someone else who is better than she.* Esther 1:19b. The king was pleased with this advice and a search began for someone to take Vashti's place. Esther was among the many maidens brought to the harem. She quickly became a favorite due, no doubt, to her beauty and her modest countenance. Like Deborah, Zipporah, and Noah's wife, God would be able to use the self-effacing Esther to do His work. Humility, we know, is a valued trait in Scripture.

Consider how one woman's disobedience allows another's obedience to provide a remedy in which God's plan can unfold: Eve/Mary and Queen Vashti/Queen Esther.

When Esther found herself in an elevated position she did not take advantage of it nor deceive herself into believing that it was her "right" or her "due." Instead, we read in Esther 2:15 that she moved cautiously and with great humility.

*When the turn came for Esther (the girl Mordecai had adopted, the daughter of his uncle Abihail) to go to the king, she asked for nothing other than what Hegai, the king's eunuch who was in charge of the harem, suggested. And Esther won the favor of everyone who saw her.*

Ultimately, Esther is made queen and her role continues to reveal itself as Mordecai approaches her with his request that she speak to the king. When we understand that this jeopardizes her very life, we fully grasp that it is no simple task. Indeed, it takes a great deal of courage for Esther to go to the king. His law was such that anyone

approaching him, without first being summoned, risked death. It is easy to see why Esther's first response was one of apprehension. It was when Mordecai pointed out to Esther that her purpose for coming to the role of queen might very well be found in halting the expected tragedy that she accepted the responsibility.

Esther 4:16 gives us her response:

*Go, gather together all the Jews who are in Susa, and fast for me. Do not eat or drink for three days, night or day. I and my maids will fast as you do. When this is done, I will go to the king, even though it is against the law. And if I perish, I perish.*

Esther reiterates for us the value of intercessory prayer, fasting, and a confidant self-approach to God. She leaves no stone unturned.

Esther had faith in the power of God, just as the woman with a hemorrhage had faith in the power of Jesus. And as did the Canaanite woman whose daughter was possessed. Both these women turned to Christ for their answer. Scripture is filled with women whose strong faith allowed healing to take place, nations to be saved, and wars to be won. Faith, Jesus reminds us, can move mountains.

As the story of Esther continues to unfold we see that she has taken on the task of warding off impending doom against the Hebrews. Through her fasting and praying, and that of her community, she willingly approached the king and was instrumental in stopping the slaughter of the Jews. We also learn that the treacherous Haman, who was the instigator of the plot against the Jews, himself, becomes the victim of his own dishonesty. God has worked all for His good and the good of His people.

Another holy woman who was able to ward off impending doom against God's people was Judith. She is certainly a favorite among many women today as having the admirable traits of beauty (remember this also indicates virtuousness), physical strength,

wisdom, and faith. The entire book of Judith (which immediately precedes the story of Esther in the Bible) is a narrative of one woman's ability to follow God, honor Him, and live completely for Him. Judith's story is replete with the message that God can work all things for His good and the good of His people as the first seven chapters of Judith make it known that in every way, God's people were facing the worst of circumstances, the ultimate of enemies. A combination of any and every terrible thing that had come upon them was magnified in the force of Holofernes' command of the situation in which God's people were literally dying of thirst and nearing annihilation.

In Judith's story we are reminded that an ego can be someone's undoing as Holofernes' own ego allows him to listen to Judith's praise of "her Lord" and easily see himself as the object of her worship. Her verbal commitment and continued affirmation of wanting to please her Lord increases Holofernes' vulnerability and ultimately is his demise. Judith, like Esther, is put in a powerful position but does not attribute the position to her own worthiness but to God's mercy and kindness and as such she is His willing instrument reminding us that we can all make that same choice; to be His willing instrument.

Mary became the perfect fulfillment of what it means to be an instrument—handmaid—of God's. Her life is witness to the ways in which Old Testament lives, symbols and lessons are the precursor for the perfection to come in the New Testament.

Both Judith and Esther are loved today in their roles as women of God and Esther's triumph is still celebrated in the feast of Purim. It reminds the Jews of the remarkable woman who was brave enough to face her own death to save God's people. She is our sister in faith as she reminds us of our own needed bravery to live our Christian faith in the face of rampant secularism. And, like Judith, Esther's complete faith in God carried her through events that seemed impossible.

She teaches us to rely on the intercession of others, the value of fasting and faith, and the need to recognize God's hand in our everyday lives. Esther's story is one of triumph and glory, just as Jesus' resurrection is one of triumph and glory over death. Her story gives us reason to be filled with faith and find strength in that faith. Her story reminds us that we are all handmaids unto the Lord and that He will work in our lives as we allow Him. There is a very real beauty in the term "handmaid" in that it represents our own understanding that we are called in a unique way to know, love, and serve God through our feminine genius.

## *The Word of God*

*When the king's order and edict had been proclaimed, many girls were brought to the citadel of Susa and put under the care of Hegai. Esther also was taken to the king's palace and entrusted to Hegai, who had charge of the harem. Esther 2:8*

*No one had a bad word to say about her, for she was a very God-fearing woman. Judith 8:8*

*Instead, whoever wants to become great among you must be your servant, and whoever wants to be first must be slave of all. Mark 10:43b-44*

*Humility and the fear of the Lord bring wealth and honor and life. Proverbs 22:4*

*God is not unjust; he will not forget your work and the love you have shown him as you have helped his people and continue to help them. Hebrews 6:10*

*Judith threw herself down prostrate, with ashes strewn upon her head, and wearing nothing over the sackcloth. While the incense was being offered in the temple of God in Jerusalem that evening, Judith prayed to the Lord with a loud voice. Judith 9:1*

*God did this so that men would seek him and perhaps reach out for him and find him, though he is not far from each one of us. For in him we live and move and have our being. Acts 17:27-28*

*Do not reprove me in your anger, Lord, nor punish me in your wrath. Have pity on me, Lord, for I am weak; heal me, Lord, for my bones are trembling. Psalm 6: 2-3*

*Judith answered him: "Listen to the words of your servant, and let your handmaid speak in your presence! I will tell no lie to my lord this night..." Judith 11:5*

*We see that through Mary – through her maternal "fiat" ("Let it be done to me") – God begins a New Covenant with humanity. This is the eternal and definitive Covenant in Christ, in his body and blood, in his Cross and Resurrection. Precisely because this Covenant is to be fulfilled "in flesh and blood" its beginning is in the Mother.*

Mulieris Dignitatem

## *Mary*

*"Blessed are you who believed that what was spoken to you by the Lord would be fulfilled."* Luke 1:45

With those words, Elizabeth confirms what we already know about Mary, the mother of Jesus: that she freely, and without reservation, trusted in God. With those beautiful words we only begin to fathom the depths of Mary's faith in God. For we know that Mary had all the reason to question and doubt the news as revealed in Luke 1:35.

*The Holy Spirit will come upon you, and the power of the Most High will overshadow you. So the Holy One to be born will be called the Son of God.*

As the mother of Jesus, we know that Mary had a tremendous responsibility placed upon her. Her future—and most certainly our future—was forever changed when she responded to the angel Gabriel, telling him that she considered herself a servant of the Lord. With the acceptance of this life-altering news Mary sets in motion a chain of events that would ultimately provide the only way in which to rectify Eve's transgression. Just as a woman freely rejected God and His will, a woman was needed to freely accept Him and His will.

And in so doing, Mary agreed to bring into the world God's answer to our sins.

Upon accepting this role, and having learned of Elizabeth's pregnancy, Mary visits her cousin. It is during this stay that we are privy to Mary and Elizabeth's brief but telling conversation. In those few lines of Scripture we see the absolute love that they share for God and for His purpose in their lives. In Mary's song, often called Mary's Canticle, she gives great praise and honor to God. She recalls His hand in the lives of His people. We are again reminded of God's love towards a humble servant, any modest servant, as Mary says,

*My soul proclaims the greatness of the Lord; my spirit rejoices in God my savior, For he has looked upon his handmaid's lowliness; behold, from now on will all ages call me blessed.. Luke 1:46b-48*

We serve a sovereign Creator. He is the Alpha and the Omega; the beginning and the end. He set us upon our course and knows the number of hairs on our head. Our Lord, blessed be He, made us in His image.

It was His choice, in His omnipotence and with great love, to choose Mary as the mother of Jesus. Mary, in that one moment of acceptance became Mary, our Jewish mother; Mary, the mother of our Savior. In her willingness to be God's handmaiden she served humankind like no other human being has ever done. She became the vessel of our salvation and pivotal to the salvation history of mankind.

What do we know about this woman chosen by God? We know that she was a young Jewish virgin when the Lord's angel approached her. We know that she grew up steeped in the Jewish faith and that this was, no doubt, essential for Christ's own upbringing. We know that she abided by Mosaic law and brought her newborn Son to the temple for his dedication.

What we may not know, we can assume. We can assume she was a faith filled young woman to have found such favor with the Lord. We can also assume that she would be humbled by the titles given her. Titles that include Holy Mary, Holy Mother of God, Holy Virgin of virgins, Mother of Christ, Mother of divine grace, Mother most pure, Mother most chaste, Mother inviolate, and Mother undefiled. Postulations and teaching abound regarding her immaculate conception and her assumption into heaven. Both of which could be interestingly supported by Jewish teachings.

But those assumptions begin to sidetrack us from what is critical for us to know about Mary. They are roadblocks to us grasping imperative knowledge about this woman, the human mother of Christ. We must look past the centuries of debate over her role in salvation history and immerse ourselves in what her gift to humankind was; and how her Jewish identity is something for us to embrace.

She makes us ask ourselves many valuable questions about the Jewish roots of Christianity and to look at it more closely, more clearly, than ever before. She can help us understand our powerful connection to the Jewish faith. Were not the Jews the chosen people, and could we not inherit the same blessings through our acceptance of the Jewish messiah? But we also must ask ourselves about the obligations that are ours to uphold with such a gift. It is no surprise that Mary gives us a role model for that as well. Her gift wasn't just in accepting her role to bear the Christ-child but also in modeling behavior of a true disciple of the Son of man.

What did it really mean to be Jewish in the years leading up the Christ's birth? What was Mary's life like as a young child? What would she have been taught, and then subsequently teach her most beloved son? What would have been His place as a young man in the household? These are the things that give our faith its building blocks because these questions take us right to the heart of Christ's life on earth.

One of the celebrations that Mary would have participated in was Passover. Also known as Pesakh, this pilgrimage festival was one of great joy and, according to Scripture, a sacred duty to uphold. According to Deuteronomy 16:14-15, God's people are called to rejoice and be together during festival times. As a young girl and then teenager, Mary and her family would have seen Passover as a triumphant occasion. Then, as the mother of Christ, Mary would have shared her Son, the final Pesakh Lamb, in the most self-giving of ways. A Son she loved and raised would be sacrificed for the salvation of all.

As a youngster at the Seder table, Mary would have heard the Passover questions in the blessed home of Anne and Joachim. Mary would have sat at Pesach dinners, listening to her father answer the questions, completely unaware of how she would, one day, be giving birth to the Son of Man who would, himself, become the lamb of the Passover dinner.

> *1. Why do we eat only Matzoh, and not any other kinds of bread, on Pesach?*
> *2. Why do we eat bitter herbs, or Maror, at our Seder?*
> *3. At our Seder, why do we dip the parsley in salt water and the bitter herbs in Charoset?*
> *4. Why do we lean on a pillow while eating tonight and do not sit straight like other nights?*

Mary would have heard that they ate matzoh to remind themselves of the time that their ancestors had to flee, in a hurry, from Pharaoh. There was not time to let their dough rise and so they baked their dough into hard matzoh, which became a symbol of their hurried flight from Egypt.

She would have been told that the bitter herbs were a reminder of the bitterness of slavery and the cruel ways in which the Jews were treated by Pharaoh and that salt water represented tears of Hebrew slaves while parsley represented new life. It was from the tears and hardships of their ancestors that new life sprung for the Jewish

people. Charoset, made from apples, walnuts, cinnamon, and red wine, had the texture of clay and was to be a reminder of the bricks that the Hebrew slaves were forced to make.

Finally, the leaning on a pillow was a reminder of freedom. In the days of slavery, only the free had the luxury of leaning on a pillow, or somehow reclining, as they ate. To make a statement of freedom, Jews will lean on a pillow during the Passover dinner.

Along with the yearly Passover celebrations, Mary would have celebrated the Sabbath on a weekly basis. These traditions would have been brought into the home of our Savior as well. He would have witnessed, every week, His mother ushering in the Sabbath as an anointed family time. The Jewish Sabbath celebration typically would have consisted of two candles being lit before sunset on Friday evening. One candle would have represented God's command to remember the Sabbath and the second candle would have represented God's command to keep the Sabbath holy. (Exodus 20:11) Jews are called to bring God's light into the world and that is the overriding principal of the candles. Jesus would have listened as His mother made the beautiful hand gestures above the flames as she spoke the blessings, "Blessed are You, Eternal One our God, Ruling Presence of the Universe, Who makes us holy with mitzvot and gives us this mitzvah of kindling the Sabbath lights."

The Sabbath, now ushered in, would have been followed with rituals that Joseph would have led. Joseph would probably have blessed his son, our Savior and Lord, and may have honored his wife, The Virgin Mary, by reading from Proverbs 31:10-31 which states, "*When one finds a worthy wife, her value is far beyond pearls. Her husband, entrusting his heart to her, has an unfailing prize. She brings him good, and not evil, all the days of her life…*" The wine then would be blessed which sanctifies the Sabbath and Mary would have been, once again, witnessing the foreshadowing of a time where her Son's own blood would be shed for our salvation. Like the Passover dinner, where Jesus' blood literally became the blood that covers us, every Sabbath has a way of reiterating that fact because

for us, every Sabbath is a celebration of His resurrection. His was the body and blood given over for our salvation.

Sabbath itself would have been celebrated from Friday sunset to Saturday sunset. Friday's meal would have been the most indicative of the celebration. Although Sabbath meals vary according to household, it would have been a kosher meal. Mary's home would have observed the dietary and ritualistic laws, as given in Deuteronomy and Leviticus. There would have been foods that were acceptable (chicken, salmon, soft cheeses) and foods that were trayf, or forbidden (mixing meat with dairy, pork, shellfish). Most assuredly, Mary would have raised Jesus honoring the laws, customs, and rituals put forth in the Torah as given to Moses from Adonai.

Jews of Mary's time also celebrated other occasions like Sukkot and Shavuot, both festivals, like Passover, that often involved pilgrimages to the temple. Purim, like Yom Kippur and Rosh Hashanah, was not a pilgrimage festival.

Sukkot, often called the Feast of Booths, is based upon Leviticus 23:34b-36, "The fifteenth day of this seventh month is the Lord's feast of Booths, which shall continue for seven days. On the first day, there shall be a sacred assembly, and you shall do no sort of work. For seven days, you shall offer an oblation to the Lord, and on the eight day you shall again hold a sacred assembly and offer an oblation to the Lord. On that solemn closing you shall do no sort of work." Sukkot is a celebration of the fall harvest and is truly a joyous celebration of the exodus from Egypt, given unto the Lord as He said to Moses, "That your descendants may realize that, when I led the Israelites out of the land of Egypt, I made them dwell in booth. I, the Lord, am your God." Leviticus 23:43.

While Sukkot was a fall festival, Shavuot and Passover were spring festivals. This is why we see, as Christians, our Easter celebration so very close on the calendar to Passover celebrations. Shavuot, also called Pentecost, was a bringing of the first fruits to Adonai. Hence,

it was a pilgrimage festival in which the Hebrews would bring to Jerusalem offerings of fruit and grain. Sukkot is a very significant event in the history of Christianity as we trace it, from its original instructions in Exodus and then Leviticus through Ruth and to our own redemption as a people outside of the covenant. It is in Leviticus 23:22 that we read, "*When you reap the harvest of your land, you shall not be so thorough that you reap the field to its very edge, nor shall you glean the stray ears of your grains. These things you shall leave for the poor and the alien. I, the Lord, am your God.*"

The great Adonai is already making a way for us to be redeemed through the laws He has set in motion because it is these same laws that Boaz, our kinsmen-redeemer, follows when he leaves enough grain for Ruth to glean. Ruth, daughter-in-law of Naomi, became the great grandmother of King David, from whose lineage Christ was born! When we say that God sees the whole picture, we aren't just mouthing esoteric words. We see, through connections such as these, that the Lord has a plan in which we are all part of, in which we are all participants with purposes to our lives. We see the plan of salvation history as it unfolds.

So, in raising the Christ-child in a household replete with Hebrew tradition, Mary most certainly pleased God. Not only did she create a household that upheld the traditions of the faith but she would have upheld the morals and values of the Jews as well. So, along with celebrations that included weekly Sabbath and yearly events like Yom Kippur, Passover, Sukkot, and Purim, Mary would have been brought up honoring such values as Shalom bayit which literally means peace of the house. Of course, we know that she gave birth to the Prince of Peace and that one of the great gifts we are given by Christ is His peace. Having been taught, by His mother, the grace of peace, it would have been quite fitting when He said to His disciples, "*Whatever town or village you enter, look for a worthy person in it, and stay there until you leave. As you enter a house, wish it peace. If the house is worthy, let your peace come upon it; if not, let your peace return to you.*" Matthew 10:11-13 As His mother honored the concepts of peace, so, too, would He have honored them.

While this isn't to say He "learned" in the strict sense of the word, from His mother, it is to say He was born of a woman who was given many graces from the Father. She was a woman who worshipped, honored, and obeyed the Creator in a way that surrounded Jesus with His Jewish faith. She shaped a house where, according to Jewish tradition, Jesus would have been exposed to prayer at an early age and his more formal home education of studying Torah would have started around age five. If we know, as Christians, that Jesus took on a human form so that we could literally "look and see" from His examples, it would make sense that He also took on human form so that His early years would have reflected what God wanted shown as well: the study of the sacred texts.

Remember that Mary presenting Jesus at the temple was a Jewish tradition. This would have been the second temple (destroyed in 70 A.D.) and was where Simeon, a righteous and devout Jew, came in the Spirit to the temple to see the baby Jesus. Simeon, holding the baby, said to an amazed Joseph and Mary, *"Now, Master, you may let your servant go in peace, according to your word, for my eyes have seen your salvation, which you prepared in sight of all the peoples, a light for revelation to the Gentiles, and glory for your people Israel."* Luke 2:29-32

Maybe our most important information about Mary is in the studying of her last words, *"Do whatever He tells you."* John 2:5

In full and complete obedience to the Father, Mary has pointed us to our salvation in Christ. As all good mothers will do, she gently encourages us on the right path with her soft spoken, yet authoritative words. Do whatever He tells you. It requires each of us to ask ourselves: What is Christ calling me to do? And in answering that we find Him calling us to love one another as He has loved us.

Mary gives us, through her acceptance of God's will in her life, a perfect example of answering God's call to holiness. She is holy in her perfection of charity, for it is through her that Christ's birth

allows for our rebirth in Him. Let her call to holiness remind us of ours as well.

Mary models for us true discipleship of Christ as well as complete obedience to the Father. With this knowledge of her character, God chose Mary to be Jesus' mother. He chose Elizabeth to bear John the Baptist and Mary to bear the Christ Child. In that way, Mary was to serve God and the greater good of God's people. Mary's life clarifies what it means to be a servant of God, what it takes to be a servant of God. She exemplifies for us how we are able to serve God through serving the greater good of all people.

Because of her gentle and unassuming demeanor, her willingness to be a "handmaid," God is able to ask anything of Mary. He can count on her cooperation. And as we know He was not asking for a small sacrifice. He was ultimately asking her to sacrifice her son for all humankind. It was a great act of love. It would certainly seem that her love for God, and even her love for us, was bigger than her heartache. This must have been the case for her to have survived such a tragedy. In this way Mary helps us see that it is possible to get outside of ourselves and serve one another in a most glorious way. However, this is both a difficult and often unrewarding earthly task.

Nonetheless, Mary calls us to do just that. She helps us see that in serving God we are helping raise humanity to a level pleasing to Him. Indeed a level planned by Him. We proclaim this in the *Our Father* prayer when we say, *thy will be done, on earth as it is in heaven.* When we mirror Mary's unselfishness, we are able to participate in God's plan for humankind in the most glorious of ways.

As well as being the one chosen to carry the Christ child, we should remember that Mary was Jewish. She most definitely would have enriched Jesus' life with the Jewish celebrations of Yom Kippur, Chanukah, the Sabbath, and Passover. From this perspective, the birth of Jesus provided a means for God to offer salvation to His own people. It then tied Gentiles to Jews in a deep and abiding way, as

Gentiles soon began to acknowledge the Jewish Messiah as the Son of God.

Our Christian faith, then, evolved from the Jewish faith and has its origins in the faith that worshipped the one true God. For us, as Christians, He is the God who sent the Son. While Christians recognize a need to claim Jesus as Lord and Savior, we also should recognize the gift we have received from the Jewish people. Jews, like Christians, have seen persecution and intolerance for thousands of years. The Jewish people held on to the belief in the one true God while pagan nations attempted to destroy and conquer the Jewish race. Through women like Esther, Deborah, Noah's wife, and Mary, the Jewish faith survived in such as way as to bring the Messiah.

Finally, we recognize Mary as one of the first disciples. As obedient as she was to God, she was also a faithful follower of Christ. She set an example for us, showing us how to live and abide in His ways. Mary shows us what true discipleship necessitates. From her life we know that, as Disciples of Christ, there will be pain and sorrow along with joy and gladness. The depth of one allows us the full exultation of the other just as the horror of the crucifixion allowed for the glory of the resurrection. They go hand in hand.

Discipleship includes times of upheaval and periods of grace. At the heart of discipleship is the transforming love of Jesus: a love that can forever change us. It is this all-encompassing love that allows us to share in each other's lives in the richest of ways. Without love, as St. Paul tells us, we are just clanging symbols. Jesus showed us, through His tender words and charitable deeds, how to love one another in a manner that pleases God. And, of course, Mary's love for the Father allowed us to know the Son, our only way to the Father. Through it all, Mary gives us a beautiful example of a discipleship that is based on such love.

Undoubtedly, there are certainly many, many things we can do in life without love. But without love, they would all be meaningless, empty acts. We might even get very far with our egos leading the

way. But nothing will change the fact that God's love, as given to us in His Son, is our only means of salvation. It all begins and ends with this devotion. It is placed before us to freely choose or reject. It is a love that Mary most certainly had.

Indeed, it was Christ's love for us that allowed Him to suffer and endure death on a cross. It was God's love for us that allowed Him to consider offering up His Son for us. And it is our love for one another that allows us to be all that God intends us to be.

Like so many women whose stories are told in Scripture, Mary gives us courage to embrace God's will with enthusiasm and confidence. She shows us that being a loving servant to God means being a beacon of light to all women. She had a unique role to fill and did so with a heart full of devotion. In saying "yes" to Gabriel she said "yes" to each and every one of us.

While Mary's gift of free will was no more, or no less, than Eve's or yours or mine; the way she used it was different, indeed. Finding herself in the most difficult of circumstances to understand, she relied solely and completely on God. In that way she becomes an example for us to do the same.

Then, as the mother of Christ, she continued to be an example of selfless love, always directing us to her Son as she did the servants at the Wedding of Cana when she said, "Do as he tells you." We honor her in her role and are grateful for her continued direction to her Son, who gives us life.

The world gives us many ways to practice greed, envy, and trickery. We live in a society that values notoriety and fame. We are encouraged to value what is **in** this world while Scripture tells us we aren't even **of** this world. Mary, then, in the most gentle of ways, reminds us the value of selfless love. Her benevolence helps us recognize that our very existence is, and was always intended to be, an expression of love.

## *A Mary Garden*

It is a Catholic tradition to acknowledge and honor the unselfish and holy life of the Blessed Virgin Mary. One way of doing that is to plant a *Mary Garden.*

In the Middle Ages, missionaries and travelers spread stories across Europe about flowers named after Mary and various times of her life. Mary Gardens that featured these flowers became popular there, and later the tradition made its way to America. Around 1932 it is believed that the first *Mary Garden* in the United States was constructed on the grounds of St. Joseph's Church in the Woods on Cape Cod.

Now, many flowers that symbolize the name of Mary grace gardens throughout this country. If you, too, would like to honor our Blessed Mother through flowers, perhaps you would like to create your own special garden spot that showcases plants that carry her name. The center focus of the garden is a statue of Our Blessed Lady. The size of the garden does not matter. In fact, people with limited space can use a small area and a few select flowers to surround their statue. If you are an apartment dweller, you can set up your Marian Garden in a window box or even use a small statue with a single flowering plant. Reflecting on Marian flowers can be a perfect starting point for meditating on the life of Christ through Mary.

To help set up a *Marian Garden,* flowers and their meanings are listed below. This list is far from complete but should give you enough information to begin.

Lily – Legend tells us that the Angel Gabriel held a lily in his hands when he came to tell Mary that she was chosen to be the mother of the Savior. Lilies are often depicted in pictures of Mary as an indication of purity and grace.

Rose ~ The rose symbolizes Mary as the Queen of Heaven. The red rose represents sorrow. The white rose shows joy, and the yellow rose stands for the honor bestowed upon Mary.

Columbine ~ This flower is often called Our Lady's Slipper. Legend says that this flower sprang from the earth where Mary's feet stepped when she was on her way to visit Elizabeth.

Violet ~ The violet is a symbol of modesty and simplicity; humble acceptance to the words from the angel Gabriel...."Let it be done unto me according to Your will."

Carnation ~ Legend says that the carnation bloomed on the night of Jesus' birth; a sign of Mary's joy at the Child's birth.

Oxeye Daisy ~ It is said that when the wise men reached Bethlehem they looked for a further sign to guide them to the new king. King Melchior saw a white and gold flower and knew which building to enter.

Star of Bethlehem ~ The shape of the flower is said to resemble the star that the Magi followed to find the Christ Child.

Snowdrop ~ The snowdrop is said to have bloomed in February when Mary took Jesus to the temple to present him to God.

Rosemary ~ It is believed that Mary hung the linens of the Holy Child on the rosemary bush to dry. Afterwards, the bush carried a sweet aroma.

Forget-me-not ~ The tiny blue flowers of this plant represent Mary's eyes.

Meadow Cress ~ This plant is called Our Lady's Smock. It stands for the fine linens made by Mary's hands. It is said that Mary learned to weave as a young girl.

Lavender ~ This fragrant plant represents purity, cleanliness and virtue – Mary's spotlessness and chastity.

Marigold ~ Early Christians placed marigolds around statues of Mary in place of coins calling them Mary's gold.

Bluebells ~ These bell-shaped flowers resemble tiny thimbles and represent Our Lady's working hands. They were often called Our Lady's Thimbles.

Speedwell ~ This plant is also known as Mary's Resting Place. A legend tells that its blossoms marked each spot where the Blessed Mother rested during the flight into Egypt.

Lily of the Valley ~ Lily of the Valley is called Our Lady's Tears. It is said that her tears fell at the foot of the cross and turned into tiny fragrant blossoms.

Iris ~ The Iris is a flower, like the Lily, that represents the Annunciation.

Herbs ~ Almost any herb can be used in your garden to represent Mary. Soothing and healing herbs represent her heavenly love and mercy. Bitter or sour herbs represent her sorrows and sweet smelling herbs reflect Mary's spiritual sweetness.

Fuchsia ~ These gently drooping flowers resemble pendant earrings. It is said that the child Jesus playfully hung these flower 'jewels' on his mother's ears.

Fleur-de-Lis ~ This is sometimes called the Ave Maria flower. There is a legend that tells of a fourteenth century knight. He was extremely wealthy but renounced his worldly possessions and entered a Cistercian Order of monks. Since he loved Our Lady very much, he would continually repeat the first two words of the prayer, day and night: *Ave Maria, Ave Maria.* Some of the monks ridiculed him for his simplicity and told him that Mary would not listen to his

unfinished prayer. He grew old and when he died, he was buried in the chapel yard of the monastery. As proof that Mary heard and loved his short but earnest prayer, a fleur-de-lis plant sprang up on his grave. On every flower shone in golden letter the words, Ave Maria. The other monks finally realized his great devotion for the Blessed Mother; and her devotion to him.

### *Novena*

A novena is prayer of repetition which lasts nine days. A Catholic who prays a novena is asking God for a favor or a blessing or help in some way or another. Ultimately, however, every Catholic who prays a novena is entering a place of full submission to God's will. God's action or inaction isn't the point of the novena; but, rather it is about that complete surrender in which you cry out "Here's what I think I want or believe will be good for me...What do you think, Father?"

A novena, rightly said, has the ability to place you in a direct, intimate relationship with God where you are able to experience His grace in ways that will deepen your love for Him while granting you strength, courage and peace for your journey. They are never mindless repetitions but a cleaving to God in trust and faith. Novenas to the Blessed Mother and making use of her many titles are often both an effective and a comforting way to pray.

Come, O my soul, humble thyself at the feet of Mary, thy Mother, and depart not till she hath blessed thee. O blessed of God and enriched with all grace, in thy clemency bless my afflicted soul, and by thy mighty intercession, obtain for me, from thy beloved Son, the object of this novena of prayer, (mention request)

Say one OUR FATHER, one HAIL MARY and one GLORY BE

# *The Word of God*

*Grace, mercy and peace from God the Father and from Jesus Christ, the Father's Son, will be with us in truth and love. 2 John 3*

*And the God of love and peace will be with you. 2 Corinthians 13:11*

*If I speak in the tongues of men and of angels, but have not love, I am only a resounding gong or a clanging symbol. If I have the gift of prophecy and can fathom all mysteries and all knowledge, and if I have faith that can move mountains, but have not love, I am nothing. If I give all I possess to the poor and surrender my body to the flames, but have not love, I gain nothing. 1 Corinthians 13:1-3*

*Then Simeon blessed them and said to Mary, his mother; "This child is destined to cause the falling and rising of many in Israel, and to be a sign that will be spoken against, so that the thoughts of many hearts will be revealed. And a sword will pierce your own soul too." Luke 2:34-35*

*But the angel said to her, "Do not be afraid, Mary, you have found favor with God. You will be with child and give birth to a son, and you are to give him the name Jesus. He will be great and will be called the Son of the Most High. The Lord God will give him the throne of his father David, and he will reign over the house of Jacob forever; his kingdom will never end. Luke 1:30-33*

*God created man in his image, in the divine image he created him; male and female he created them. Genesis 1:27*

*David built houses for himself in the City of David and prepared a place for the ark of God, pitching a tent for it there. 1Chronicles 15:1*

*Come and see the works of the Lord, who has done fearsome deed on earth. Psalm 46:9*

*Christ is the bridegroom of the Church – the Church is the Bride of Christ.*

Mulieris Dignitatem

## *Mary Magdalene*

From start to finish, Mary Magdalene seems to be the quintessential female for today's Christian woman. Of course that may seem a bit absurd to people who view her life as one of sin or as a prostitute; however, we know that Jesus came here for sinners and we know that Jesus came here looking to forgive sins. Maybe most importantly, we know that Jesus came here looking for believers and she believed unequivocally. Scripture also lets us know that Mary Magdalene helped support Jesus' ministry and was so faithful that she followed Him to His crucifixion. Finally, she was the one to whom He chose to show Himself upon His resurrection. And so, it seems as if we have a lot to learn from her.

Early on we learn from Eve's story the reality of sin and the need for repentance. Mary Magdalene seems to embody that message. She accepted Jesus' forgiveness and freely chose to follow Him. Like many women are unable to do, it seems as if Mary Magdalene found a great ability to move forward in Jesus' healing and forgiveness. She did not look back but instead kept her focus on Jesus' teachings and the courage that gave her to forge ahead. According to Scripture, she was also interested in helping others know and accept Him. We find, in Luke 8:1b-3, that Mary Magdalene, Joanna, and Susanna had been cured by Jesus and were, in fact, supporting Him in His ministry.

*The twelve were with him, and also some women who had been cured of evil spirits and diseases: Mary (called Magdalene) from*

*whom seven demons had come out; Joanna the wife of Cuza, the manager of Herod's household; Susanna; and many others. These women were helping to support them out of their own means.*

Along with supporting Him during His mission on earth, Mary Magdalene was also at His death. She stood at a distance during the crucifixion and was there as the earth trembled and rocks broke apart. She must have heard the centurion exclaim what she already knew in her heart, *"Surely he was the Son of God!" Matthew 27:54b.* We have to admire her bravery as well as her faithfulness. We know that many followers feared for their lives and thus avoided the scene at Calgary. Her story reveals to us the power of complete faith. It allows us, in the face of whatever difficulty we might have to confront, to be able to replace fear with hope and courage. And as we know, His death did not stop her devotion. It was Mary Magdalene who prepared spices to anoint His crucified body.

Not only was she a devoted follower of Jesus' but her trust was so deep, so strong that she is to whom the Lord appeared upon His resurrection! She was the first to acknowledge, accept, and witness to our Risen Lord.

When we consider that our faith rests upon the Lord's resurrection, and it was to Mary Magdalene that He chose to first appear, we know that she must be a role model of the faithfulness for us. Throughout the Old and New Testament faith, like wisdom, is a valued and sought after trait. When we look at all the ways in which women used their God-given gifts to know, love and serve God we can see how important it is for women to not lost sight of the importance of those gifts. We see how imperative it is that women follow their own feminine genius so that their portion of God's divine plan will unfold.

Indeed, when we go back and consider how God knew that Noah's wife would be up to the arduous task on the ark, or that Zipporah would trustfully support Moses, we have to assume that He also

knew Mary Magdalene had the faith to witness His Son's resurrection.

When we hear the recounting of Mary Magdalene, Joanna, and Mary (the mother of James) sharing their knowledge of the risen Lord it seems evident why women were chosen for this momentous occasion. We see that aspect of the feminine personality that can be almost overwhelmed with emotion! Feelings, as von Hildebrand shares, are often dismissed as inferior to intellect or as having the ability to make one less respected when following them at the sake of all else. However, von Hildebrand goes on to say that while there certainly are those sorts of feelings that ought to be harnessed, addressed, and corrected, there are also the sorts of feelings that derive from a Divine source—and those feelings need to be valued and respected. Specifically, she writes:

*"If the feelings vibrating in their [women's] hearts are noble, appropriate, good, legitimate, sanctioned, and pleasing to God, then they are precious jewels in God's sight."*

We have to assume that Mary Magdalene's "feelings" through Christ's ministry where the kind that von Hildebrand spoke of—the kind that were precious jewels in God's sight—and the kind that produced good fruits. As we know, the women then tell the eleven apostles their experience at the empty tomb but were not believed. Only Peter ran to see if there was any truth to their tale. The other men considered the story "nonsense." As much as these men loved and followed Jesus, we have to wonder what their responses might have been at the empty tomb. In this interesting exchange we come to see how men and women must work together for the Lord; each bringing his or her own piece to the intricate puzzle of life. We see in these moments after the Resurrection the true, divinely-intended complementary nature of the male/female relationship.

Certainly it has been our experience that women, as mentioned in the earlier section, "Holy Spirit," have a particular intuition in which the Lord works with them. This doesn't presume that men are

without gifts in which they, too, work with God. More pointedly, it restates that women have a connection to God in a different manner then men. And we should never underestimate how much God depends on both relationships: male and female.

This simply reiterates the fact that when we get caught up in a secular message that calls us to aspire to, as equals, all that men pursue, we might lose sight of what God wants us to seek. And we will also lose sight of how God wants us to do our seeking.

In retrospect we clearly see that a faithful woman was able to receive the Risen Lord and witness to disbelieving—or at least typically cautious—men. But then, upon accepting this fact, these same men were able to go into the world and spread the Good News in ways that were probably unavailable to women. This understanding allows us to welcome God's plan with knowledge that each and every one of us will play a necessary and vital part in the building of His kingdom.

Together, men and women are able to bring to this world the message of eternal life with Christ. This reality teaches us all to be hopeful, jubilant and tenacious. Indeed, our belief in the salvation of Christ, and its accompanying joy, is the biggest banner we can wave.

The way we live, the attitudes we take into the world and the light we reveal is the most significant testament we can give as we persevere in life. These aren't things we keep sequestered in our hearts but are, instead, realities that we bring into the world. What Jesus tells us in Matthew 25:40 should guide our everyday lives.

*The King will reply, "I tell you the truth, whatever you did for one of the least of these brothers of mine, you did for me."*

So in Mary Magdalene we have a very real example for today's Christian woman. She gives us conviction to accept Jesus' forgiveness and to courageously follow Him. We are encouraged to

be all that we can be through His gift of salvation. As the first witness to His resurrection, she inspires us to be the faithful witnesses that He calls each of us to be, both in our hearts and in our lives.

## *The Word of God*

*Early on the first day of the week, while it was still dark, Mary Magdalene went to the tomb and saw that the stone had been removed from the entrance. John 20:1*

*At this, she turned around and saw Jesus standing there, but she did not realize that it was Jesus. "Woman," he said, "why are you crying? Who is it you are looking for?" Thinking he was the gardener, she said, "Sir, if you have carried him away, tell me where you have put him, and I will get him." Jesus said to her, "Mary." She turned toward him and cried out in Aramaic, "Rabboni!" (which means teacher). John 20:14-16*

*Mary Magdalene went to the disciples with the news: "I have seen the Lord!" John 20: 18a*

*Be joyful always; pray continually; give thanks in all circumstances, for this is God's will for you in Christ Jesus. 1 Thessalonians 5:16-18*

*Jesus turned and saw her, "Take heart, daughter," he said, "your faith has healed you." And the woman was healed from that moment. Matthew 9:22*

*Then Jesus answered, "Woman, you have great faith! Your request is granted." And her daughter was healed from that very hour. Matthew 15:28*

*For Christ has redeemed all without exception.*

Mulieris Dignitatem

## *Scripture's Messages*

From Eve to Mary we look at women of Scripture and extract their messages to us. They teach us that God's blessings are boundless and that when we use our free will to both accept the salvation of Jesus and offer up our repentant hearts, we live lives most pleasing to God. We see that we will experience a variety of seasons, all working for the good of His plan. There are times when we will be strong and times when we will be weak. Through them all we are able to serve God and our reason for living.

We understand from Eve the consequences of sin and from Noah's wife the need to serve God and others in a joyful and diligent way. Sarah teaches us to turn impatience and jealousy into gratitude and faith in God's promises. She shows us the very human characteristics of envy and anxiousness and allows us to bask in God's commitment to us when we are less than what He would like us to be; thus, encouraging us all the more to be godly women.

Leah's life and place as a powerful Matriarch of the faith calls us to look at how our lives were meant to glorify His kingdom. In tuned to the Spirit, Leah teaches us to develop those same gifts of the Spirit that allow us to answer His call.

Lot's wife reminds us that it is harmful to give our future to the past and rob God of our "today's." Rebekah's story instills in us the need for intercessory prayer while Rachel's strength gives us encouragement to call upon God with our own needs and desires. Shiphrah and Puah remind us of God's natural law placed upon our hearts and the rewards for responding to it.

Zipporah challenges us to respond to God's call even when it is in stark contrast to what we have imagined for ourselves and to cherish the ways we might support our loved ones in their own journeys. Deborah shows us how to yield power in a way that is pleasing to God and yet productive in our earthly existence. Ruth, a Moabite woman, foreshadows our own purchase by the blood of Jesus Christ.

From Miriam we continue to see that even in the midst of God's graces we are able to fall prey to earthly temptations of envy and ungratefulness. But, also as importantly, we see from Miriam how powerfully we can serve God when we inspire and encourage one another.

Esther helps us wield whatever power God has given us for His good and the good of His people, our brethren. Mary, the mother of Jesus, was the embodiment of the love that God looked for in humankind. She is the role model of discipleship and a link to our sisters in faith. Mary Magdalene renews our understanding of why Jesus became man: to forgive our sins and to give us eternal life.

All women in Scripture, from those named to those unnamed, show us how we are uniquely called to honor God, Jesus, and the Holy Spirit all our days.

## *Living Your Faith*

Along with your morning offering, create a list of statements or questions that you can use to begin your day in Christ. Restate the questions for an end-of-day examination of conscience.

Look at the examples offered here—for a starting point—and then add to them or create a whole new list most specifically relevant to your personal journey. Consider journaling each day to track your "progress" as you continue to connect with your past and live your faith more fully today.

- ✓ What is He encouraging me to do?
- ✓ Who is in my life and for what reason?
- ✓ How can I serve Him today?
- ✓ Am I allowing something from the past to hold me back from serving Jesus today?
- ✓ Do I have a grateful attitude?
- ✓ Do I encourage and welcome the guidance of the Holy Spirit?
- ✓ Am I persevering with faith in Him?
- ✓ Do I enthusiastically embrace my feminine genius?
- ✓ Am I joyfully pursuing my purpose?
- ✓ Do I spend enough time in silence so that I can be more fully aware of God's call upon my life?

______________________________________________________

______________________________________________________

______________________________________________________

______________________________________________________

______________________________________________________

______________________________________________________

______________________________________________________

______________________________________________________

______________________________________________________

Ask the Holy Spirit to reveal a Scripture verse to you and write that verse here:

Consider why this verse "speaks" to you and record your personal revelation.

Brainstorm a list of adjectives that describe feelings you know you must now give over to God in order to continue on your journey. Ask God to show you what you must now turn over to Him. They are roadblocks that are ready to be torn down. During your next quiet time with God, read your list to Him. Ask Him for deliverance from these impediments. Prayerfully trust in Him.

Consider ways in which your trust in God ebbs and flows. Write a journal entry about this and ask for His hand in helping you overcome any obstacles that are in your way to a fully committed relationship with Him in which you are able to give praise even in the absence of that for which you may long.

Today I made a difference. I honored the Word of God when I...

First, be on the watch for a time where your words are better left unsaid. Second, be on the watch for a time where your words can be of the encouraging, inspiring kind that will reveal Christ's light and love to the world. Record your experiences.

You are redeemed through Jesus Christ, your savior. Ruth was redeemed by her deep and abiding love for Naomi. Throughout the week, find ways to show your own abiding love for the people in your own family and, in doing this, remember that you are showing your own abiding love in Jesus who dwells in all. Record some of your feelings this week, as you live in tenderness, so that they will remind you of the depth of the affection Jesus has for you.

CPSIA information can be obtained at www.ICGtesting.com
Printed in the USA
LVOW121431111211

258892LV00001B/127/P